In Praise of For the Love of Vietnam

Kat Fitzpatrick's *For the Love of Vietnam* is simply a great read. The historical context is made vivid by the juxtaposition of her family's experience in Saigon during the final days before the fall of Saigon. The final scene, reminiscent of the ending of *Schindler's List,* is sure to leave readers with tears in their eyes.

– Paul Block, author of *Song of the Mohicans*
and 15 other historical novels

Much of the writing about America's involvement in Vietnam has been from the military/political point of view. Missing from that body of work is an account of what life was like for American expats in the country. In her new book, *For the Love of Vietnam*, Kat Fitzpatrick brings readers a fresh perspective.

In the summer of 1974, at the age of eight, Kat arrived in Saigon with her parents and six siblings. Here is an account of a family adapting to the harsh reality of Saigon living, her father's work as a CIA operative running a clandestine radio station broadcasting propaganda into North Vietnam, and their heroic escape as the doomed country was falling apart. Through personal letters, poignant memoirs, family photographs, and published material, Fitzpatrick constructs a compelling narrative through which readers will better understand the scope of the Vietnam problem.

– Karen Kaiser, author of *Gardens in the Midst of War*
(publication pending), librarian, Phoenix Study Group 1974-75

It is rare to read a fresh perspective on history, especially from an eight-year-old girl. Kat Fitzpatrick was a child in Vietnam during the last years of the American occupation. Her fresh and previously unheard memories are enriched and augmented by her father's (James Welch, CIA Operative) many journal entries, letters from and to his wife, interviews, sidebars, and so much more. The gripping subject is the 1975 brilliant evacuation of over 1,000 House Seven propaganda radio station personnel, orchestrated by Kat's esteemed father. The purpose is to bring this courageous and nearly impossible feat to light. Kat has given a factual, conversational, and stellar glimpse into an aspect of the American War in Vietnam to all who were and have been affected by it, and all who dare to know. Thank you, Ms Fitzpatrick!

– Nanson Serrianne, MSE
(Masters of Science, Education)

For the Love of Vietnam

For the Love
of Vietnam

A war, a family, a CIA official,
and the best evacuation story never heard

Kat Fitzpatrick

Published by Quarter Turn Studios
For more information or to contact the author, visit kat-fitzpatrick.com.

ISBN (paperback): 979-8-9885811-0-9
ISBN (ebook): 979-8-9885811-1-6

Names: Fitzpatrick, Kat, author.
Title: For the love of Vietnam : a war, a family, a CIA official, and the best evacuation story never heard / Kat Fitzpatrick.
Description: Albany, NY : Quarter Turn Studios, 2023.
Identifiers: ISBN 979-8-9885811-0-9 (paperback) | ISBN 979-8-9885811-1-6 (ebook)
Subjects: LCSH: Vietnam War, 1961-1975--United States. | Ho Chi Minh City (Vietnam) | United States. Central Intelligence Agency. | Propaganda, American. | Evacuation of civilians--Vietnam (Democratic Republic) | BISAC: HISTORY / Wars & Conflicts / Vietnam War. | POLITICAL SCIENCE / Propaganda.
Classification: LCC DS556.93.F58 2023 (print) | LCC DS556.93.F58 (ebook) | DDC 959.704--dc23.

Cover art and photograph by Kat Fitzpatrick
Cover design by M.V. McLaughlin
Library of Congress Control Number: 202391132

First edition 2023

Published in the United States

1 2 3 4 5 6 7 8 9 10

For my family.

And to all those affected by the Vietnam Era.
In other words, all of us.

CONTENTS

May what I've created serve to open minds
to understanding,
open doors to healing conversations,
open eyes to seeing what was and what could be.

My Father's Plaque

For many years of my youth, I would walk past a wall of fame on the way to my parent's bedroom. Sometimes I would stop and examine what was hanging there and ponder the stories behind each item. There were framed letters, a few photos, a big telegram, and this plaque. Each item said that my father had done something. Done something big. But I knew him as just my good ol' dad and though I somehow knew *of* the stories portrayed on the wall, I don't remember ever hearing them told. It's as if I learned that he was in the CIA and rescued 1000 people by virtue of some cultural osmosis rather than by way of celebration or commemoration.

Thus it was that I inherited a great deal of archival "footage" that echoed with meaning but was not imbued with it. I guess, after all, that's what this entire book—and all my Vietnam writing projects, are about—stringing together all the little pieces, weaving them into a fabric that tells a cohesive story.

Of all the things on the wall, this plaque stood out—for its wood veneer, its shield-like shape, and the brilliance of the brass plate, long since faded. The words were impactful and also poetic and their meaning felt way beyond my grasp but they, like a good poem, would not let me go.

Even today, I have found a new element in the verse. I had always assumed that the "Year of the Rat" referred to the year the evacuation took place but that year—1975—was actually the year of the Cat in Vietnam (Rabbit in China). The co-worker,

To James Welch
The Year of the Rat

Within An
Accelerated
Timing Factor You
Helped Activate
A Motivational
Implementation
Program Through
A Coordinated
Approach On An
Orchestrated
Basis With All
Deliberate Speed.

Cam On [Thank You],
Chuc May Mam [Good Luck]

who gave my father this plaque, must have known my father's birth year and included the zodiac sign to commend the qualities of his personality.

Those born in the Year of the Rat are known to be clever, optimistic, and successful. Also, according to Vietnam Online, they "have the ability to climb over a tall wall or run across the roof" without falling. Or, perhaps, it could be said, "activate a motivational implementation program through a coordinated approach on an orchestrated basis with all deliberate speed."

Kat Fitzpatrick
April 28, 2023

"When it was all over, I was never sure whether or not I was going to get an award or a good kick in the ass."

Major Jim Kean, USMC
Last Men Out | Epilogue
30 April 1975

NEAR DEATH

They were just about there. Just about safe.

But just as James E. Welch, CIA operative, was about to breathe a sigh of relief that he and those under his care had made it to safety, an armed soldier approached from the naval checkpoint and shot out rapid-fire orders in words Welch could not understand.

His translator, Giang Ngoc Dinh, stepped forward. The message he relayed to Welch was earth-shattering. Apparently, no orders had been received allowing them to leave the beach. No matter that Welch's operations assistant had just left with his own group of 600 and were now on their way to safety. He and his group of 400 were suddenly sitting ducks, trapped ashore, easy targets for any soldier or wayward soul that wanted to strike out in spite. With the military situation of South Vietnam falling to pieces faster than anyone had ever expected, it was quickly becoming an every-man-for-himself scenario. But there was still a possibility of escape. There had to be.

"Tell them we *do* have permission," Welch said in low tones. Above all, nothing must set the soldiers off.

Nevertheless, the angry guard and Giang exchanged several heated sentences. Both were members of the South Vietnamese Army, but Giang was poised to exit

These Landing Craft Utilities (LCU) are similar to what was used to evacuate the residents off the beach of Phu Quoc on April 29 and 30, 1975, in one of the last official evacuations of the war.

the doomed country while the other was on the verge of being abandoned by the Americans who had promised, over a decade before, to protect the world from the evils of communism. And now they were running. What right did they have to live? What could possibly keep a forsaken soldier from killing them now?

Inexplicably, the head guard chose to put off the moment of fate. He motioned to a subordinate, sending him in search of news from the commanding officer. Sweat dripped down Welch's back as they waited. He could feel his group's gazes upon him, the weight of their lives on his shoulders.

The young man returned all too soon, his face a mask of anger. No one could find the commander in charge. Rumor had it that he had left the jetty in a motorboat, fleeing with his family just after the first group had departed. When Giang translated this, Welch's heart dropped. The delicate thread of control was quickly fraying. Without the usual rules of order in place, the situation was in danger of spiraling out of control.

The guns that stood between my father and freedom were M16s which the US Military has provided in large numbers to the South Vietnamese forces. They had become a standard in the 1960s, an upgrade from the wood-based rifles that had previously defined warfare.

Should that happen it was quite possible that they could be slaughtered where they stood. They were so close to escape and yet worlds away.

Before Welch could form a reply, another truck pulled up and a dozen more stone-faced South Vietnamese soldiers poured out of the covered bed and ran toward them. The head guard barked out a command and the troops quickly fell into formation in front of the two getaway boats.

Welch eyed the M-16s clutched in the hands of the uniformed men. He had never seen anything look so menacing. Their barrels were lowered toward his people, all those House Seven employees he had promised to get out. The tiniest wrong move would end in disaster and there was no help in sight.

IN HONOR OF THOSE
WHO SERVED

When you enter the Washington D.C. National Mall
from 21st and Constitution Avenues, the Vietnam
Veterans Memorial is invisible; it sits sunken in the wide
green lawn as if harboring a truth too difficult to bear.
When I arrived on a muggy August morning in 2014,
my heart beat like a drum—I was not a sight-seeing
tourist, but a sort of pilgrim, a writer seeking benedic-
tion, and my chances for that seemed as unclear as the
profile of my obscured destination.

My decision to write about Vietnam had begun in
a time of personal difficulty. The circumstances of my
life had been precarious—I'd unfairly lost a job due
to illness, I was staying temporarily in my son's college
housing, and I had little-to-no savings. And, despite the
overwhelming conviction that I must write my family's
Saigon stories, I did not want to presume to overwrite
or circumnavigate the stories of the American soldiers. I
simply could not continue to write about the war without acknowledging them—many of whom had been
sent alone and unprepared to serve in the same country
where I had spent much of my eighth year.

I willed myself forward along the concrete path,
my camera gripped in a damp and trembling hand.

(following pages)

The Vietnam
Veterans Wall draws
you in, compels you
to participate in the
War's impact.

MILLER · MICHAEL ... JOHN ... MICHAEL J ROMANKO ...
· BOBBY LEE SPENCER · ... MICHAEL ...
· LAWRENCE W BREITNITZ · ROBERT E WILLIAMS · KENNETH C SPENCER · JOHN M TANNEY · DONNIE B SANTELMAN ...
DENNIS L GILES · STEPHEN E BREINER · GEORGE M CUNNINGHAM · THOMAS J SWOJCINSKI · JOE C BERTA ...
· WILLIAM T DAVIS · WILLARD F MORELOCK · ALLEN W INGRAM · NORMAN N ... INGHAM · KENNETH ...
JAMES E PENNINGTON Jr · ARLON G SCHAEFER · JERRY McCONNELL · LOUIS ... KEV · CHRISTOPHER ...
· SAMUEL F ANKNEY · JOSEPH H THOMAS · JOSEPH K SEARLE · DARWIN H NIEMEYER Jr · MICHAEL A ...
MICHAEL D McNAUGHTON · RICHARD G WOLFF · THOMAS N TRAINHAM · MICHAEL R TROUT · PAUL J SUBLE ...
· ERNEST L ROWE · JAMES B COLLINS · DENNIS K BLAIR · SAMMY BURROLA Jr · WILLIAM A CA ...
· MARK A ELLSWORTH · ROGER A FULKERSON · RONALD L DELVERDE · LARRY GENE DROWN · JOHN W EA ...
· DONNELL HOWARD · JOHN A JENKINS III · TERRY F GRAJEWSKI · RANDOLPH C GRIMES · DAN ...
· JAMES H MORGAN · WILLIAM H PALMER · NORMAN M PAULSEN · HERBERT POK DONG CHO · HA ...
· CURTIS L BATTON · JOSEPH W SEBASTIAN · EVERETT H SMITH Jr · MICHEL K SUBLET ...
· ROBERT V BOLLMAN · FREDERICK E BORCZYNSKI · JOHN L BOYD · ANDREW T BUKOVINSKY · GEO ...
· WILLIAM F LEMOINE · FREDERICK J CARLSON · BENJAMIN F CASTANEDA · GEORGE M CO ...
· MICHAEL D ECKERFELD · ALFRED A FILIPPELLI · BARRY K FISK · DOUGLAS E GOSS ...
· JAMES D HACEK · DANNY C HAYES · JAMES R HEARD Jr · MAURICE H KINREAD · RICHARD A LARRICK ...
· GREGORIO MENO CAMACHO · NICHOLAS P LESANDO Jr · LARRY L LOWER · DALE A LUSTER · DARRELL L LUTRICK ...
· LEE ROY McELHANEY · BARRY A OLSON · RANDALL A OLSON · JEROME OVERTON · DOUGLAS A PAGE ...
· LARRY E WRIGHT · CLARK E PEDEN · JACK A PLUCINSKI · OSCAR K PORTER Jr · JAMES R PRUETT · STEVEN P RANCE ...
· DAWSON J ATWOOD · TERRY D RATLIFF · JON A RIPPEE · ARTURO B RIVAS · CARLTON ROSS · JOHN A RUSCITO ...
· CHARLES R SLUSSER · GEORGE J SMITH Jr · JOHN C SMITH III · JOHN W STAHL · JOHN W STATES ...
· JOHNNY W THOMPSON · MICHAEL J TOBEY · STEPHEN L TOWNSEND · FREDERICK E TRANI Jr · RONALD D WILLS ...
· JOHN C WALLACE · RICHARD B TROTTER · JAMES W WEBB Jr · WILLIAM A WESTLAKE · JOSEPH G AMBROSIO ...
· LAWRENCE B BANEK · MARK A BARNES · JEFFERY C NILES · TOMMY RAY BOWMAN · DERRIS BROWN ...
· GEORGE A CARTER · DAVID K CHAHOC · DELFIN H COOK · JAMES W CRAMER · RICHARD DAVIS Jr ...
· CHARLES E DE LASSUS · JERRY E DENSON · DONALD L ELDRIDGE · MITCHELL L FIRMIN · RONALD L GRANVILLE ...
· PAUL D GROSICK · KEVIN L GREENE · PAUL HOLSTON · QUENTIN F HURST · TYRONE JACKSON · LAWRENCE R MEISCHROD ...
· LEROY A KING · ROBERT E KNOLL · EDWARD L LAWTON · CHARLES J L MASON · GORDON W OGILVIE ...
· BLAINE S MILES Jr · ANTHONY J MONTOYA Jr · JAMES A MORRIS Jr · LUTHER C BERRYMAN · LARRY J SMITH ...
· JOHN L JOHNSON · DAVID H PITTARD · ISHAM I QUICK · PHILIP D REEDER · ROGER A VICKERT · VIRGIL J WEB ...
· WILLIAM A SMITH Jr · EFRAIN SOTO Sr · HERBERT G TAYLOR · GARY D COLLINS · WILLIAM T DECKER ...
· JOHN A WOOD · BRADFORD D WRIGHT · WALTER C BLANTON · ROBERT L HAMILTON · AUSTIN W HAVERKAMP ...
· DAVID L DIXON · RAYMOND E EVANS · DAVID P HALPIN · DAN B NORTON · RONNIE L POUNDS ...
· CARL V HANSEN · ROGER L JOHNSON Jr · JOHN R KLOTZ · JOSEPH D LILLY · CARL R USSERY · LYLE G BROOKS ...
· FREDERICK E ROUSE · CLIFTON SPILLER · GERALD S STOZEK · TERRY P BRADY · TERRY B DAY · LARRY DURHAM ...
· ALEJANDRO BIRRI BAGASOL · STEVEN R BINKLEY · RONALD T BLEACHER · FRANCIE DAVIS · ROBERT K HAMILTON ...
· ARTHUR B CREWS · WERNER C BROWN II · GORDON BUTLER · SHERWOOD D RIKES · LEE M HALSTEAD · DAVID L SAGE ...
· WILLIE GENE GADDY · JOHN E GIBSON · RICHARD O GULLISON · FRANK E LEWBERRY · EDWARD L MACE ...
· JERRY LEE HARRIS · HAL K HOWELL · RONALD J HUELSKAMP · WAYNE E SHEPHERD · GEORGE LANGLIN ...
· JOHN J MATUSKA · MERLIN E MILLER · WALTER L MOORE Jr · BLAINE J SHEPHERD · SAMUEL M GOLEA ...
· WILLIAM C PERDUE · STEPHEN B PUGH · WILLIAM P ROLLINS · CARROLL W WHITE · JIMMY T FULLER · JERRY JONES ...
· JOHNNIE L VAUGHT Jr · WILLIAM A VOSS · CECIL B WAGNER Jr · BOBBY J BROWN · GENE NEWBERRY ...
· GENE A LAUER · PHILIP S BANCROFT · ROBERT J BARRY · PHILIP A BEASLEY · JOHNNY M FIEZEL · JAMES G NEWBERRY ...
· LOUIS V DAIGLE · JOHN DALTON · WALTER J HOWARD Jr · CLIFFORD W MARTIN · JAMES GENE NEWBERRY ...
· ULYS F HAMILTON · ALBERTO HERNANDEZ-VELEZ · CHARLES A HOLBROOK · THOMAS C MARTIN · TIMOTHY D TOWNSEND ...
· KENNETH W MILLER · GLENN R LAWFIELD · RICHARD L McCLAIN · FRANKLIN L McPHAIL · GARY R TOWNSEND ...
· DAVID L JUDY · MICHAEL D McCLAIN · HARRISON B SHAUGER · GARY R SHEPPERDSON · ROBERT E ASHER ...
· JOHN J QUICK · FREDERICK P RHOADES · RICHARD W LAZICKI · RONALD STUCKY · GERALD E SUBLER · GARY R TOWNSEND ...
· HOWARD H SMITH · DOMENICK A SPINELLI · HAMP E ZORNES · RONALD ALICEA · TIMOTHY G AKENS · RONALD D WELLING ...
· TERRY J VAN RENSELAAR · ALLEN P BROOKHUIZEN · JAMES D DAVIS · ALLEN TON · HENRY JONES Jr · MONTIE THE PERRY ...
· CHARLES A BRANCH · RICHARD B CLEMENTS · GARY W BROWN · LEMUEL JOHNSON · JOHN W ENGLISH ...
· ... FERGUSON Jr · ... KRAUHS · JOE R LAURENCE · ROCCO ... VICTOR PEREZ ... · KENNETH ...

I descended into the scrape in the lawn, and the mirrored wall of carved names overshadowed me. I came to a quick halt. A dozen yards in front of me was a man pressing his hand to the slick black marble, his head back, his eyes searching for a name. His grief was palpable, and not wanting to intrude, I silently captured the image from a distance. As I reviewed my photos, he departed and I had to hurry to catch up. My voice quivered as I asked permission to use the picture and told him a little bit of what I was doing and why. He nodded as I spoke, as if in approval.

"People can't forget," he said. "They have to remember. There're a lot of names on that wall."

"That's why I'm writing about it," I said. "To remind people about Vietnam."

His wife said, "His buddy was three days from coming home."

My eyes stung, and though I felt ashamed to be the one near tears when he was the one who had borne the loss, I extended a hand. The veteran graciously took it, his grip comforting and gentle.

"Thank you for what you are doing," he said.

"I'll do my best for you, sir. I'll do my best." As our hands parted, I could not help but feel that I had received the blessing I had been so earnestly seeking.

I do not often write about the battlefields and those who fought—my stories are about other times and other places—but the thought of the veterans stays with me, their experiences and their sacrifice always present. I hope my work honors them and bolsters a renewed interest in what that undeclared war represents to our history and to our future.

Veteran John Granfors seeks his buddy's name. His friend died just three days before he was due to return from Vietnam.

PART ONE

MAN ON
A MISSION

END OF A NATION

On April 30, 1975, Saigon, the capital of the Republic of South Vietnam, was extinguished like an ancient flame.

In the weeks leading up to that day, as 18 heavily armored divisions of the North Vietnamese Army closed in on the city, panic filled the streets, the homes, and the offices of Americans and South Vietnamese alike. After 10 years of fighting the northern communists, the fear of their arrival was palpable.

On April 3, CIA officer James E. Welch, chief of a clandestine radio operation, kissed his wife and kids good-bye. They boarded a plane to safety while he stayed behind to maintain business as usual.

That was his assignment, but he had other plans.

A quintessential
Saigon scene, 1960s

Tòa nhà số 7 Hồng Thập Tự

HỒ BƠI
NGUYỄN BỈNH KHIÊM

TRƯỜNG CAO ĐẢNG
QUỐC PHÒNG

ĐẠI HỌ
VĂN K

AFVN
ĐÀI TH QUÂN ĐỘI MỸ

THVN9
ĐÀI TH VIỆT NAM

VỊ TRÍ TÒA NHÀ
TƯƠNG TRỢ ĐẠI HỌC
QUỐC TẾ BỊ ĐÁNH BOM

ẦN
IOA LƯ

GETTING OUT YESTERDAY

James Welch had every intention of following on the heels of his wife and family as soon as possible, but he wasn't about to leave alone. For nearly three years he had been the operations chief, a father figure of sorts, for a group of South Vietnamese employees at Mother Vietnam, a PSYOP radio program that broadcast anti-communist propaganda into North Vietnam.

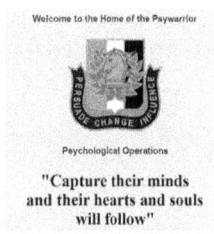

Welcome to the Home of the Paywarrior

Psychological Operations

"Capture their minds and their hearts and souls will follow"

Propaganda planning is a continuous process requiring imagination and determination.

– www.psywarrior.com

The operation was housed in an old building fondly known as "House Seven" because it was located at 7 Hong Thap Tu Street. Although it was associated with the CIA Headquarters at the American Embassy just down the road, it was classified as "super-secret" and not easily identifiable to the average passerby.

Still, the North Vietnamese spy network was at least as active as the CIA's, and the radio station had been infiltrated more than once by Viet Cong passing as ordinary Saigon citizens. So James Welch's staff—all of whom he felt a personal obligation to protect—knew what it would mean if the city was taken by the enemy. Their identities were not safe. They would be called out as American sympathizers. There would be little hope for survival and drastic action would have to be taken. As the star of the show put it: "If the communists take

(left)

"Jim's place [House Seven, 7 Hong Thap Tu Street, top left of photo] is guarded but not overly so as no one is supposed to know what is going on inside."

over and we can't get out, my father will shoot us and then commit suicide."

There was no better motivation than certain death, and Welch took the situation in hand and began tactical planning to get his people out "yesterday."

"Your husband may be shot by the bureaucracy," he wrote to his wife the day after she and the family departed, "but I intend to get my people out regardless of the consequences."

So far I am doing almost all this on my own and your husband may be shot by the beauracracy but I intend to get my people out regardless of the consequences. I spoke to Hoa tonight and will take her and Duc and Amin (if he can get here) on my ship——or at least get her on the list of people to be taken out. She is resigned to die at the hands of the VC but I don't think that should be necessary. I will talk to Mr. Di later. Talk now is of getting 1 million people out. I don't believe it. They may try and then cry and say we are sorry. I am not operating that way. I may fail, but I intend to do what is necessary before the crunch comes and succeed. There are many details I can't write here for obvious reasons. If we make it, it will be an odessy worth writng a book about— if we don't make it it still w *all my love to every*

James Welch's letter home on April 4, 1975, 26 days before the end.

There was only one problem. The U.S. embassy in Saigon had a huge investment in making it look as if the Vietnam situation was doing just fine—and while they had let his family out, they weren't planning on letting any U.S. government employees go anywhere, not Americans and definitely not South Vietnamese. It was going to take a clever, if not devious, sleight of hand to get his people out. Luckily, Welch was trained in exactly that.

(right)

The Mother Vietnam gray propaganda radio program operated in Saigon's "super-secret" station, House Seven.

Mother Vietnam was one of five propaganda radio programs that were broadcast out of House Seven, beginning shortly after the Paris Peace Accords of January 1973. Soon after wrapping up the Paris talks, the distinct programs, each operating on a separate frequency, were nurtured into being. These stations were intended to put pressure on the North Vietnamese and the Viet Cong to abide by the terms of the cease-fire and hew toward pro-democracy attitudes.

WHITE, GRAY, AND BLACK RADIO: DEFINITIONS

The colors white, gray, and black refer to the types of propaganda utilized.

> ➤ The source of white propaganda is acknowledged and truthful.
> ➤ The source of gray propaganda is not acknowledged but no attempt is made to hide the origin. It may or may not be truthful.
> ➤ The source of black propaganda is never acknowledged. Thus it may appear to come from other sources and is seldom truthful.

A great deal of work went into each of the daily shows, which were broadcast from early 1972 to the end in April 1975.

Instruments of all kinds were used in the programming.

Music and shows were recorded and performed live right from the House Seven studios at *7 Hong Thap Thu* Street, Saigon.

The official crest of the CIA.

CIA employment application.

The CIA—the Central Intelligence Agency—was created in 1947 as the new peacetime intelligence service. It replaced the OSS, the Office of Strategic Services, which had been established after the bombing of Pearl Harbor on December 7, 1941.

Employees of the CIA often referred to their employer as "the company" and were sent all over the world to gather intelligence, or information, in order to keep the country safe.

CIA MISSION STATEMENT

According to CIA.gov, CIA employees are "the Nation's eyes, ears, and sometimes, its hidden hand . . . their mission is to pre-empt threats and further U.S. national security objectives by:

➢ Collecting foreign intelligence that matters;
➢ Producing objective all-source analysis;
➢ Conducting effective covert action as directed by the president; and
➢ Safeguarding the secrets that help keep our Nation safe."

STANDARD FORM 57—NOV. 1947
U. S. CIVIL SERVICE COMMISSION • **APPLICATION FOR FEDERAL EMPLOYMENT**

Intelligence Research Specialist GS7

Foreign Affairs Officer GS-7

Washington, D. C.

James Earl Welch

1000 Otis St., NE

Washington, 17, D. C.

TRAINED FOR
PSYCHOLOGICAL WARFARE

James Welch had become a spy for the CIA early in 1952 when he was recruited by "the company" shortly after graduating with his master's in History and International Affairs from Catholic University in Washington, D.C. He was likely sought after because he had been singled out as having a proclivity for German during his college naval military training during World War II.

The only son of George and Edna Welch of Middletown, N.Y., he entered military service in 1943 through the V-12 program, a successful effort to both train officers and to fill the colleges and universities that were suffering from a lack of enrollment due to the high number of enlistments.

But becoming an officer was not in the cards for him. According to his younger sister, Jean Williams, "What happened was they perceived that he had a real affinity for language, so they put him in an accelerated German program. He knew something was wrong, so he went to his commanding officer and said, 'I'm not in the navigation class, what's going on?' They told him, 'It's okay, not to worry.'"

However, when he sat for his final exam, the one that would promote him to a naval ensign (equivalent to a second lieutenant in the Army), he found himself at a great disadvantage.

"It was awful," said Jean. "He had to take a test on things he'd never learned. He was so smart, he figured most of it out but he missed passing by one tenth of a percentage point.

"My parents went up to see him commissioned—and he wasn't. It was a horrible and sad day. He took his uniform in his arms, rode a public bus, and went to turn it in."

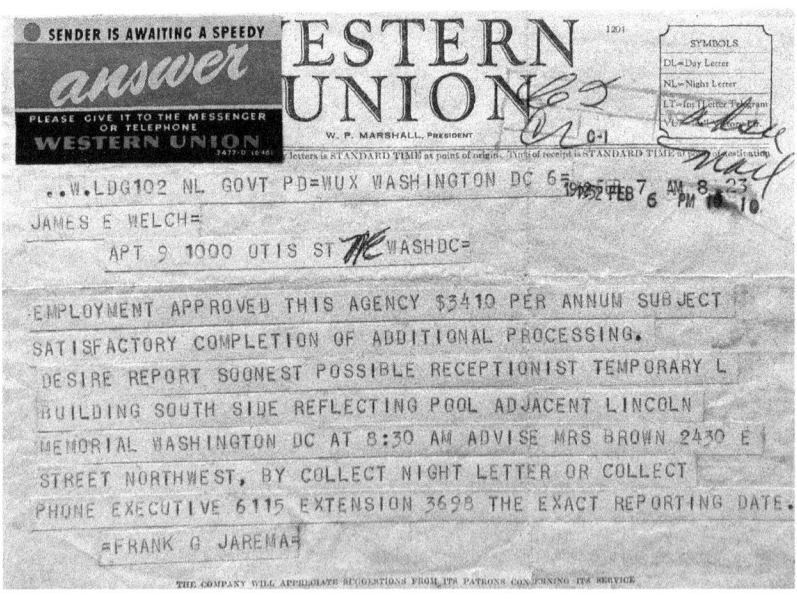

Fortunately, said Jean, her brother's optimistic and philosophical nature won out over despair.

"So, then he was a regular Navy man and was assigned to New Orleans, where he worked as a carpenter," she said. "That was a happy time in his life. The pressure was off—he'd bombed out and he could handle it."

Had he passed his officer's test, he would have likely remained in the Navy and never filled out the typewritten application to be a "Foreign Affairs Officer" at the CIA. As it was, when he was hired by the Intelligence Agency, he was sent to Munich in 1956, where he worked undercover in East Berlin. According to a CIA colleague, Leo Small, they were there to clandestinely assist with German intelligence gathering.

"We were in the same unit," he said. "We were both there in liaison with the German service, okay? The official name of that office was the *Bundesnachrichtendienst Bundes*: Federal, *nachrichten*: sort of 'intelligence,' and *dienst*: service. "We had regular offices," Small said. "Ostensibly"—he stressed the word—"working in the civilian field."

Welch was reassigned back to Washington in September

Passport Stamp,
1957

(left)
1952 CIA
Acceptance Telegram

1962, where he became more and more well-versed in psychological warfare—more colloquially known as propaganda. This expertise garnered him another long-term overseas assignment. This time in Korea beginning in 1970, in operations overseen by National Security Advisor Henry Kissinger. He was to head up the intelligence agency's broadcasts into communist China. Welch's pro-American programs were meant to sway citizens of the Middle Kingdom toward a greater affinity to their Cold War enemy in the West. According to English author and teacher John D. Claire, China's relations with the U.S. were rock-bottom before the '70s.

"For the Chinese Communists, America embodied capitalism and imperialism. After 1970, however, as China's relations with the USSR continued to be strained, relations with the United States (to the surprise of the world) improved," he wrote.

This may have come as a surprise to the world,

January 20, 1972
letter home:

Still don't know our future plans–it will take a while! It appears Jim's particular activity has to be decided upon by Mr. Henry K– ! And he is a very busy man. After Nixon's visit to C. [China], a decision should be forthcoming.

Well, what did you think of Pres. Nixon's visit to Peking? I guess you saw more of it back home than we did here nearby. We say his landing and reception but I don't think I say any TV after that. There is not too much more to report from Seoul right now so I will close and stick my nose in a book for a while---sound familiar?

perhaps, but most likely not to Welch, who very well may have had a hand in the pro-American propaganda being sent out from Seoul toward Peking (as the Chinese capital was known until becoming more commonly known as Beijing in the late 1970s). His success was so great that reports and recommendations were sent high priority—"by packet"—to Washington, gaining a

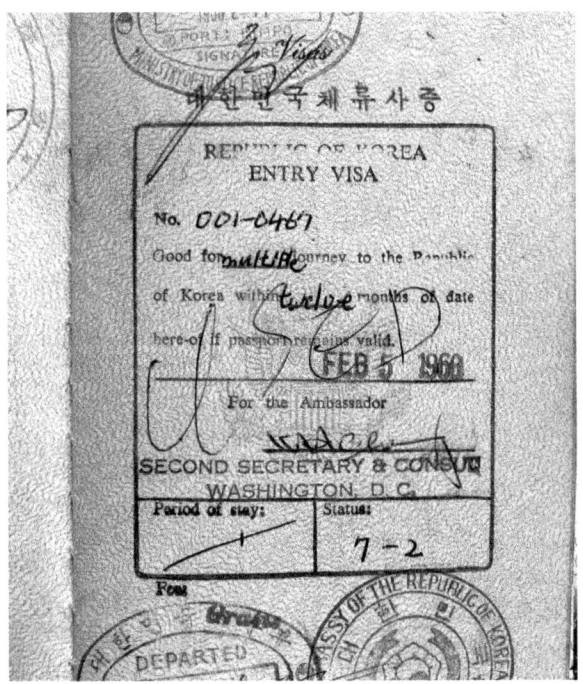

In a March 9, 1972 letter to his mother, Welch mentions the China trip but does not indicate any involvement. Was that just him being his "spy" self?

Welch worked around the globe on many assignments I never heard about.

"Spies don't keep diaries."
– *Charles Taber*

commendation from Kissinger himself.

Ironically, he worked himself right out of a job. Within two years of his efforts, relations with the old enemy had thawed so much that President Richard Nixon flew there, becoming the first U.S. president to visit the People's Republic of China since its establishment in 1949. At the Shanghai Communique, on February 28, 1972, the Chinese and U.S. governments agreed to work toward the "normalization" of relations and so, Welch's broadcasts from Korea ceased.

Thus, Vietnam. It actually came as no surprise that he was reassigned to Saigon. It was a duty no overseas CIA officer could avoid in those days. At the time, Vietnam had the largest CIA presence in the world and was still a military hot-spot despite the ongoing peace talks between the North and the South.

Though it was an inevitable assignment, Welch took it up with some zeal, feeling that his talents were sorely needed.

> "In 1972 Nixon went to China so Jim had to close down his long-running Chinese broadcasts . . ."
>
> – SGM Herbert A. Friedman (Ret.), psywarrior.com

(right)-

President Richard Nixon and his wife Pat Nixon visit the Great Wall during their diplomatic trip to China in 1972.

The V-12 Program

James E. Welch as a young naval officer candidate, circa 1945.

In December of 1942, the V-12 program was established jointly by the U.S. Navy and Army. It took the form of two new college training programs which would provide tuition-free college to candidates with officer potential.

By the beginning of 1945, the program had produced nearly twenty percent of the officer strength of the Navy. By the time the program concluded in mid-1946, it had graduated 60,000 Navy and Marine Corps officers, including 38 future admirals and 20 future Marine generals."

Undoubtedly, my father had hoped to be one of those future officers. As it was, there were other things in store for him.

The V-12 program sent students to different undergraduate programs in various universities. This helped the school fill seats during the World War II years when so many young men and women were serving directly in the armed forces. This list shows the various locations my father studied during his enrollment in the program. Note, however, that the last site was not a school but the naval base in New Orleans, Louisiana.

Service (vessels and stations served on)

ONOP N.Y., N.Y.

NAVY V-12 UNIT HOLY CROSS COLLEGE WORCHESTER MASS

NTS RMS PRINCETON NEW JERSEY

USNTS GREAT LAKES ILL

REC STA NAV REP BASE NOLA

Henry A. Kissinger

Henry A. Kissinger was the nation's 56th Secretary of State from September 1973 to January 1977 and the 7th National Security Advisor from January 1969 to November 1975, serving both Presidents Nixon and Ford.

His role in shaping the face of our country's foreign policy is lauded as nothing short of legendary, so commendations from him certainly shine a bright light on Welch's work. However, Kissinger was also a controversial statesman often seen cheek-by-jowl with Nixon, whose legacy is marred by corruption and whom my father had no great love for.

Secretary of State Henry A. Kissinger kept his finger on the pulse of what was going on in South Vietnam.

Still, Kissinger did shepherd several significant global shifts including the recognition of China in 1972 and the much-yearned-for withdrawal of U.S. troops from Vietnam in 1973.

He was awarded the Nobel Peace Prize for the latter accomplishment, in tandem with his North Vietnamese counterpart Le Duc Tho, who did not accept it on the grounds that, despite the signed agreement, the peace had not actually been attained.

"We believe that peace is at hand," Kissinger had said at a White House press conference on October 26, 1972.

That proved not to be the case as history has revealed. To his credit, after the true end of the war, Kissinger attempted to return the award and donated the entire proceeds to the children of American service members killed or missing in action in Indochina.

STALIN'S GHOST AND
THE LOVE OF VIETNAM

In hindsight, it's easy to recognize what a mess Vietnam was. It's an easy thing to say that James Welch should not have been so worried about the threat of communism. But can we really imagine what it was like to have come of age in the time of Hitler and the Nazis? To have been influenced by McCarthyism and the Red Scare?

All things considered, it's easy to think that he should have packed his bags and given up on the question of Vietnam sooner rather than later, certainly long before the U.S. pullout in 1975.

However, even if he could have left the Intelligence Service that quickly—for a spy that would have been tantamount to desertion—he was loyal to his country and staunch in his quest to defeat communism, a conviction born of the commonly held belief in the Domino Theory. That theory held that should Vietnam fall to communist rule, the rest of Asia would quickly follow—and perhaps the rest of the world, too.

Again, at that time there was good reason to fear communism. Soviet dictator Joseph Stalin had killed 20 million of his own citizens between 1929 and 1953, and Mao Zedong, the Chairman of the Communist Party of China, had killed 45 million of his own people

"Is this Tomorrow? America Under Communism!"

1950s Red Scare propaganda comic book by F. Robert Edman (Author), Francis McGrade (Author), Charles Schulz (Illustrator).

between 1958 and 1962. Their legacies hung in the minds of Western policymakers like tattered red banners.

"I was fighting the ghost of Stalin," Welch said, by way of explaining his dogged fight against the North Vietnamese Communists.

But there was more to his persistence than the fear of a communist takeover. That is, he loved South Vietnam.

"Maybe I am just reflecting the exuberance of the season," he wrote home early in 1974, "but especially right now I feel a very great closeness to Vietnam and the Vietnamese people—from the ragged kids in the streets to the elegant ladies I see in the cathedral at mass to the great talents I meet every day at the studio."

The "season" he was speaking of was Tet, the Vietnamese New Year celebration, which can last as long as two weeks. One Monday, he arrived at work to find the revelry had not ended the Friday before as he'd expected—there was an uproarious street celebration outside House Seven. Much to his surprise, a group of his employees surrounded him, steering him around a big truck decorated with a huge papier-mache dragon, through the dancing and drumming revelers, and into a radio control room where they began to shower their blessings upon him. Nguyen Dung, one of the four "Vietnamese Beatles" (the most famous band of musicians in those days), grabbed his hand and made a long speech wishing him and his family good fortune.

"Naturally, I didn't understand a word of it and thought I would never get my hand back," he wrote.

"Even though I don't know much more than '*hai, mot, ba*' in Vietnamese I have been taken as a real friend by so many of these people that I'm nearly overwhelmed—especially since there are so many that I can't converse with at all. In that, I sort of feel like JFK when he told the people in Berlin: '*Ich bin ein Berliner.*'"

He began his commitment to Vietnam out of fear of communism but ended up being committed "up to his chin" to the cause of the people he was fighting for. He admitted to being an eternal optimist and would not entertain the thought that his efforts there were wasted. "They are a great people," he wrote, "and I will not concede one inch to the communists."

His dedication was only bolstered by reports that confirmed that communist troops were becoming more and more dispirited and that more and more were defecting to the South. Whether this intel was accurately portrayed was a question that would arise over the next year's challenges but he believed that his propaganda was having a decided effect on the North Vietnamese GI's but feared they would run out of time.

"Some come across, having listened over a period of time to our special peacenik appeal," he wrote to his sister. "We are wearing them away, but will it be soon enough? I don't know. I do know it has got them worried because they are attacking us in their press. And that is always a sign you are hurting them. Oddly, it is our particular selections of music that seem to bother them most. The teens up there like rock and jazz as much as kids anywhere and have taken to growing their hair long. That sends the Communist leaders right up the wall! Well, history will tell."

peacenik
/'piːsnɪk/

noun · derogatory · informal

1. a member of a pacifist movement.

History has revealed many reasons why this effort was not destined for success. However, Welch strongly believed in his mission from the beginning, and he put all his energy toward designing radio broadcasts that he believed would convince North Vietnamese soldiers to lay down their arms and return to the one true mother, Mother Vietnam, communist-free South Vietnam.

While he was in love with his job and heartened that his radio operation was expanding while many other embassy efforts were being economized or cut altogether, he struggled with the separation from his family. His wife and seven children had been sent to live in the safe haven of Taiwan while he worked in Saigon.

"I have the job I like better than any I have ever had or ever expect to have again," he wrote home early in the separation, "and the personal circumstances are the most unacceptable ever. I miss you so much. Well, for better and for worse, it will all come to an end."

(right)

The Domino Theory dominated political thinking in the 1950s and 60s.

The Domino Theory was a Cold War policy that suggested
a communist government taking root in one nation would
quickly lead to communist takeovers in neighboring states,
each falling like a perfectly aligned row of dominoes.

It was Republican President Dwight D. Eisenhower (1953-1961)
who first put forth the thought. At an April 1954 news conference, he explained that, "When you have a row of dominoes set
up, you knock over the first one, and what will happen to the
last one is the certainty that it will go over very quickly."

Eisenhower's message was clear. The United States could not
allow Ho Chi Minh to take over South Vietnam. The fall of
South Vietnam would inevitably lead to Communist expansion
throughout the rest of Southeast Asia, and thus the rest of the
world.

President John F.
Kennedy in Berlin,
June 26, 1963.

In his famous anti-communist speech of June 26, 1963, in West Berlin, President John F. Kennedy meant to say, "I'm a Berliner." What he ostensibly said was, "I am a jelly doughnut" and that is what Welch was referring to when he said he felt like JFK.

Kennedy's blunder came from saying *"Ich bin ein Berliner"* in which he used the German indefinite article *"ein,"* which supposedly changed the meaning of the sentence from "I am a citizen of Berlin" to "I am a Berliner." Herein lies the joke because a Berliner is essentially a jelly pastry.

In similar fashion, Welch had just as tenuous a grasp on the local language; his statement that he doesn't know much more than *"hai, mot, ba"* was in error. One, two, three in Vietnamese is actually: *"mot, hai, ba."*

Luckily for both men, there were competent and good-natured bilingual translators on hand who helped them through their language trials, leaving no one the worse for wear.

THE QUESTION OF WIFE
AND FAMILY

James Welch's wife was one Nancy L. Rabdau, a vivacious party girl he met when she'd arrived in Munich, Germany in 1958. She'd landed a position with fellow CIA agent Leo Small, whose office that just happened to be across the hall from his.

Her path as a CIA secretary had begun the year before during her sophomore year at Gonzaga University when, according to her best friend and sister-in-law, she had become "less enchanted with school and a bit more enchanted with her academic advisor."

Fortunately, her advisor, in an act designed to protect his career and gently redirect the feisty young woman, had steered her away from further schooling and toward the nation's capital where she could embark on new and exciting adventures. When the opportunity for an overseas post became available, she did not hesitate but wrote home to her parents in Idaho that she was on her way to Europe.

Small described her as vivacious and full of energy. "She was a very good secretary, very fast," he said. "She was very pretty, very smart, and very socially active."

It wasn't long before she'd caught the eye of Welch and after a half-year's whirlwind romance, the couple got hitched. They had two wedding ceremonies, one on August 2nd in a church with the covert "company" members, and a smaller civil wedding on August 25th with those who knew them as ordinary government staff.

Within a decade, the family had grown to include six children, and Nancy, of course, was no longer employed by "the company" but was a full-time mother and housekeeper. She threw herself into the role the best she could, deftly juggling the endless tasks and activities of a large family. She was still up for adventure and she took the 1970 transfer to Seoul, Korea in stride. Amid family activities, making new friends, and exploring the countryside, she found time to volunteer for various aid organizations. One assignment had her head-over-heels in love with a new baby. She wrote home in late 1970 about the blessed event:

> "We were only to watch her for a couple of days but once she arrived we could not let her go. Jim has already signed papers to adopt her ... We all decided to call her Kimberly Marie as she looks like a little Kim—full Korean and beautiful! We all love her and pray there will be no hitch in the adoption ... send a prayer it will all work out—we'd feel like we were losing one of our own if we had to give her up."

Tours of duty for CIA personnel are often short-term like much of the military. In 1972, there was a great deal of speculation about whether the family would be able to stay on in Seoul for another much-hoped-for additional year or be called back stateside.

The orders came suddenly at the beginning of the summer: James was to report to Saigon—and because South Vietnam was still considered a war zone—the family was to report to Taiwan to take up residence in safe government housing on Grass Mountain just north of Taipei.

Though in the beginning both Nancy and Jim Welch had felt like the luckiest people in the world to have met each other, separation and the shadow of war creates a particular kind of stress.

Fortunately, Nancy was granted a pass to visit her husband several times in 1973 and early 1974. She met his friends and co-workers, one of which was the vivacious radio star of Mother Vietnam, Mai Lan. Nancy couldn't help but love the personable young woman but noticed the favor the deejay curried with all the American personnel—she was included in every social gathering and event, from welcoming visitors such as Nancy to meeting officials from Washington. With her flawless command of English and her bright smile and charming manners, she represented South Vietnam well and gave people an image of Vietnam to which they

> Mai Lan was an instant hit with the boys on the front line— and with her American sponsors as well.
>
> – Frank Snepp

could not only relate, but feel great affection for. She was not a woman anyone would soon forget.

Thus when Saigon was deemed safe for families in 1974, Nancy was all too happy to pack up the children and make the move to the capital of South Vietnam: If James was committed to the cause of South Vietnam without his family, wouldn't he be that much more empowered when his loved ones were there to support him?

Mai Lan – the power behind Mother Vietnam

James Welch and Nancy Rabdau were married in Munich, Germany on August 2, 1958. Coincidentally, their wedding day was exactly six years before the Tonkin Gulf Incident, which catapulted the U.S. armed forces more deeply into Vietnam. Then, 56 years later, I would unwittingly visit the Veterans Memorial in Washington D.C. on the very weekend of their anniversary.

It wasn't until I was in high school that I finally asked my mother. "Why did you take all of us into Vietnam, anyway?"

Her reply was simple: "No one knew what was going to happen."

In Get Out Any Way You Can, Charles Taber wrote that early in 1974, Saigon was considered safe enough so that families could be reunited with those stationed in the city. The question of who made that determination remains unanswered but it was most likely Ambassador Graham Martin who worked extremely hard at making the war situation seem better than it ever was.

Nancy on the Saigon River during an early 1974 visit to see her husband in Saigon.

(far right)

It was no small feat moving a family with seven children around Southeast Asia. After moving in July 1974 we had a shorter than planned stay in Saigon. The Welch siblings (l-r): Chris, Jimmy, Kim, Mike, myself, Michelle, John.

"Saigon was not to be a family post for long," Taber continued. "The year 1974 saw the cease fire severely tested as Hanoi pursued its 'war in peace' campaign of continuous attacks wherever they found Saigon forces vulnerable."

Indeed, it did not take long for the signs of war to show themselves to us. But we were already there and vulnerable to the blind optimism that was already inherent in the city.

Pan Am was a popular airline in the 1970s and many of their jets carried American citizens to safety before the airport was bombed on April 29, 1975.

PART TWO

A FAMILY
ADVENTURE

1974: SAFE FOR FAMILIES

James E. Welch (1924-1992) was my father and Nancy L. Rabdau (1936-2004) was my mother and while this is their story, it can't help but be my story also. My siblings and I were moved to the doomed city of Saigon in July 1974, less than 10 months before the end. I was shuffled there as the fifth-born in a gaggle of seven kids and became one of the few American children to see the city through innocent and bewildered eyes in that fateful time.

Our relocation there was just one small part of the Embassy's plan to keep up appearances. It was a plan that had two very different sides. On one hand, it was meant to convey confidence in the Vietnam situation. If families were moving in, there was no reason to worry about any rumors of instability—it was safe for families! On the other hand, if families were returning to South Vietnam, then it was worth sending more congressional support to bolster the country's own military. This was no small thing as there was reliable evidence that the South Vietnamese Army needed at least one billion dollars to remain solvent.

This anecdote echoes the larger Vietnam picture. That is, how our nation, following the relative glory of World War II, entered into the trap of Vietnam, with misguided intentions, erroneous convictions, and absolutely no understanding of our North Vietnamese enemies nor even of our South Vietnamese allies. "Quagmire" is a word often associated with the Vietnam Era, and for good reason. The era, the war, and its lingering effects are a deep and complicated miasma we have not fully emerged from.

The end of the war was announced on January 27, 1973, when the Paris Peace Accords were signed. The treaty, entitled the "Agreement on Ending the War and Restoring Peace in Viet Nam" theoretically established a ceasefire between all concerned parties: the United States, the Democratic Republic of Vietnam (communist North Vietnam), the Republic of South Vietnam, and the Provisional Revolutionary Government of the Republic of South Vietnam (the Viet Cong, or South Vietnamese communists). However, at its essence it was not truly designed to create a lasting peace, but to give the U.S. a seemingly graceful exit strategy. The agreement allowed for American troops to depart but did not provide support or protection for the South Vietnamese Army, known as the Army of the Republic of Vietnam (ARVN). Additionally, the North held quite a bit of territory in the South, taken by force during the preceding years. The agreement did not require any communist or Viet Cong troops to pull back to the North. This "checkerboard approach" left the South at a decided disadvantage.

But the agreement allowed the American people to

The signed "Agreement on Ending the War and Restoring Peace in Viet Nam."

(Text of the Agreement signed by the Democratic Republic of
Viet Nam and the United States)

A G R E E M E N T

ON

ENDING THE WAR AND RESTORING PEACE

IN VIET NAM

The Governement of the Democratic Republic of Viet Nam,
with the concurrence of the Provisional Revolutionary Government
of the Republic of South Viet Nam,

The Government of the United States of America, with
the concurrence of the Government of the Republic of Viet Nam,

With a view to ending the war and restoring peace in Viet
Nam on the basis of respect for the Vietnamese people's fundamental national rights and the South Vietnamese people's right
to self-determination, and to contributing to the consolidation
of peace in Asia and the world.

Have agreed on the following provisons and undertake to
respect and to implement them.

exhale a sigh of relief; the troops were coming home and they could begin to put the war behind them. When President Nixon brightly proclaimed, "The people of South Vietnam have been guaranteed the right to determine their own future," it made perfect sense to Americans who believed in the God-given right for every individual to pull themselves up by their bootstraps, but this glib statement only sparked outrage for the South Vietnamese who really understood the situation.

One ARVN officer was horrified. "We were absolutely furious about the agreement. It was an injustice, more a death sentence for us than a peace agreement. We had never seen anything more illogical."

The U.S. was washing its hands of the Vietnam saga as if it were the Lone Ranger riding off into the sunset, leaving a job well-done when the truth was exactly the opposite.

The facade was well-played, however. When Nixon addressed South Vietnamese President Nguyen Van Thieu on live television, the lies seemed so plausible. "Mr. President, we have been allies in a long and difficult war, and now you can be sure that we stand with you as we continue to work together to build a lasting peace."

Secretly, Nixon assured Thieu that he would respond with the full force of American air power if the cease-fire was breached by the Communists. Thieu happily believed this, unaware that Nixon's *modus operandi,* his bull-in-a-china-shop tactics, were about to come home to roost in Washington.

Just five months after the signing of the agreement, in June of 1973, Kissinger would admit he didn't think the cease-fire would hold. The Communists were still flexing their military strength in the South and expressing their discontent with the South Vietnamese administration. That administration, led by Thieu, was notoriously corrupt—ruling not through democratic means as much as through favoritism and bribery. Ironically, the communist north protested against the South's approach to governing much more loudly than anyone in the United States did. The West's only criteria for the leader seemed to be that he was *not* a communist and therefore Thieu fit that bill to a "T."

Speaking of corruption, the U.S. Capitol was seeing its own fair share. By early 1974, the Watergate investigation—in which the Republican party was accused of a June 1972 break-in to the Democratic

President Richard Nixon and South Vietnam's President Nguyen Van Thieu are shown before meeting in San Clemente, CA on April 2, 1973. Both presidents were forced from their positions by charges of corruption.

National Committee headquarters in the Watergate Hotel in Washington D.C.—was in full swing and Nixon was being strongly implicated in collusion and the obstruction of justice. The charges were undermining his political advantage at home and dispersing any energy he had for supporting a precarious political and military situation in the Far East.

The turmoil in Washington and the grisly situation on the battlefields for the South Vietnamese soldiers was not unbeknownst to my father, ensconced though he was in an air-conditioned radio station in the heart of Saigon. Though he was not an avid supporter of Nixon—and actually believed that historians would look back at the obscure historical footnote of Watergate as a "fantastic curiosity symptomatic of our times"—he saw the attack on the President as an attack on the United States, likely fomented by communist leaders around the world.

"Their psychological warfare is much better than mine, I must admit," he wrote in February 1974.

He was also convinced that his propaganda could still make a difference for the South Vietnamese suffering on the battlefields.

"Have you heard we still have a war going on here?" he wrote to his sister. "I have to smile (grimly) when I read in the paper that the death toll in Northern Ireland has now reached a thousand over four years. We hit that in three weeks with peace having reached this favored land."

The author (age 8) and her father on Vung Tau Beach, 1974

In fact, over twenty-six thousand South Vietnamese

soldiers and citizens died in the two years after the cease-fire was signed—nearly half as many casualties as America had suffered in seven years, from 1965-1973. Intelligence estimates put Northern losses at five times higher than the South in those same two years, but they were showing no signs of complying with the cease-fire. The South was losing the peace in 1974 and there was no end in sight.

However, there was just enough intel being gathered from the field that could be construed as positive. Therefore, it was used as a tactic to declare the capital of South Vietnam as "safe for families." Thus it was that my father enthusiastically wrote to me in April 1974:

> You will, indeed, be moving to Vietnam to be with me after school is over. I think you will like it here. It is much hotter than Taipei most of the time. But still it is a very interesting place . . . It should be a great adventure for all of our family.

Some forty years later, a retired marine would blanch at the thought of our family relocating to the hot spot of Saigon at that juncture.

"There were no American troops left in the city to protect civilians," he said. "It was the most dangerous time to be there."

Excerpted from my first childhood journal

I have six brothers and sisters. From the top going down is first of all Michelle, she is warm, loving, intelligent, and humorous. She is about 5 foot 1 inch with black hair, brown eyes, and is beautiful. If I ever have a problem, I ask her and she'll understand. She enjoys life to the fullest and has taught me how to, too. (I'm not as good as her yet.)

The next in line is Chris. He is very smart and is cute with feathered-back hair and muscles. He uses *chacos*–they are two more or less sticks of about 1 and a 1/2 inch in diameter, chained together. They are a weapon and he can use them too.

Mike has curly hair like an afro, sorta green eyes and a regular body build. He is creative and smart. He likes to get his own way. He is humorous and funny.

Then comes John who has light brown-black hair, with a tinge of orange-red. He has a firm body build and is getting better-looking every day. He's fun to talk to. He is organized and neat.

Michelle

Chris

Mike

John

Jimmy is next. He often acts like a fool. But he gets good grades and is really concerned with school. He is strong and athletic. He has a short temper and a sense of humor. He will grow up good looking.

Now comes Kim, who is adopted. As of now, she is the youngest and the family beat (sic). I think she is beginning to change though. She is nice when she's in a good mood. Her real problem is she always expects too much of everybody at any time or mood.

As for me, I like to read, to write, to laugh, smile, be happy, dance, joke around, go to movies, daydream, and I especially like horses. I also like music, rock–hard and pop, country and just soft sleepy music. I like the outdoors and nature. It fascinates me.

Carla (Kat)   Jimmy   Kim

(photos by Yvonne Rabdau Alexander)

In November 1972, my father wrote to my mother's parents about the prospect of an agreement being reached in Paris the following year:

> We're keeping fingers crossed that the current build-up here plus the continuing air force pressure on the commies will put the GVN [Government of South Vietnam] at such an advantage that they will not lose the peace.

In some ways, at this time, it would be better to scrap the talks and push for surrender. Our reports are that many of their units are so weakened and morale is so bad that additional pressure could cause a collapse. But that doesn't seem to be in the cards. Whatever the official U.S. line, I feel complete support for Pres. Thieu in getting the NVA [North Vietnamese Army] troops out of here and in rejecting a coalition.

President Gerald Ford meets with Secretary of State Henry Kissinger, Army Chief of Staff General Frederick Weyand, and Graham Martin, Ambassador to Vietnam, in the Oval Office on March 25, 1975.

The commies are really something. By every measure of military and political warfare they have lost, but they keep on talking as if they had won. Well, Peking [Beijing] and Moscow appear to realize they [North Vietnam] have had it and I hope Henry the K pushes them to the wall in Paris.

In contrast to the intel my father was receiving, Kissinger did not seem inclined to show President Thieu any favor. In fact, in a secret negotiation meeting in Paris between Kissinger and Le Duc Tho on December 20, 1973, Kissinger didn't even include a South Vietnamese representative. He did let Ambassador Graham Martin sit in, so that he could brief Thieu after the fact. In other words, President Thieu had been completely sidelined and was not even included in the signing of the "Agreement on Ending the War and Restoring Peace in Viet Nam."

Is it possible that the incongruity of what my father was being fed by way of intel and the political reality was a factor in his decision-making about the evacuation? Did it help him as he was deciding to begin his clandestine efforts to stage an evacuation that Ambassador Martin would not approve of?

Motorcycle brigade proceeds down Cong Ly Street, Saigon to celebrate the South Vietnamese Army's victory at Hue.

On the left is the fenced-in Duc Hotel where my father lived while we stayed in the safe-haven of Taiwan. (Photo by J. Welch)

JULY 1974

Things started out well enough it seemed. We were
given a warm welcome by my father's people, and my
mother, a consummate traveler, was thrilled to be in
Saigon; her eyes lit up as we drove through the crowded
streets.

"This city is fun," she said. "The lights and the atmosphere are so nice."

Upon arrival, she described our assigned house
at 90A Ly Quan Tran Street as "quite beautiful" but,
because it still needed quite a bit of work including
the installation of air conditioners, a telephone, and a
washer and dryer, we decided to stay with our father at
the midtown Duc Hotel, conveniently located just a few
blocks from the American Embassy.

The CIA had turned the six-story building into quite the residential complex—heavily fortified with barbed wire and sandbags though it was—complete with pool, restaurant, and movie theater.

On our first night there, I looked out our fourth-floor window to see a Vietnamese man walking along the sidewalk below, just outside the high steel fence, a shadow in the saffron haze of the streetlight. He had a gun propped on his shoulder.

"What's he doing?" I asked from a cozy pile of pillows on the couch.

"He's a soldier," said my 13-year-old brother Chris. "There's a curfew, if you go outside right now you'll be shot."

I stared at the man, just a few stories below me, separated by only glass and my parents' protection. I wasn't afraid then. I wasn't anything. I was just trying to figure out what kind of adventure we were on, after all.

We didn't stay at the Duc Hotel for long, it was just too cramped with the nine of us; the "togetherness" was driving us all up a wall. My father, feeling inundated after two years of living a bachelor's lifestyle, was more than happy to order up a few Embassy cars to transport us and all our luggage to our new home just a few blocks away.

As I trailed after my siblings through the wide front door into the cool interior of the three-story house, I took note of the high ceilings and the tile floors, which gave the house a spacious feeling. But I couldn't help but notice that I felt hemmed in by the windows. I could not quite see through them; they weren't glass but a droopy, opaque plastic.

I opened another set of French doors and was delighted to find a small central courtyard. The house was shaped like a big square doughnut and in the center was a small blue fishpond right under the patch of open sky. It was empty now but maybe it could be filled; that would be fun.

Chris followed me into the courtyard. I pointed to the plastic coverings on the door.

The entrance of the Duc Hotel in 1967. The gun-toting soldier I saw on this sidewalk on my first night there was the first clue that I had moved to a place vastly different from the green fields of our Taiwan home.

"How come they're such ugly plastic, and not glass?" I said.

"In case of bombs," he replied. "They won't shatter."

I stared at the wilting material. After a moment's thought, I decided maybe that was okay. At least glass wouldn't fly everywhere, "in case of bombs."

Little did I know it then, but I was acquiring a new skill. One that would be tested over and over during our nine months in Vietnam. I was quickly learning how to "normalize" a situation, that is, to conjure up a sense of safety when there was none.

◆ ◆ ◆

Despite the pressing demands of unpacking, home repairs, and managing a staff of three maids, one driver, and several armed guards for the front gate, my mother managed to get most of us kids enrolled in the Phoenix Study Group which held summer and school-year classes for the 250 elementary and middle-grade Americans in the city at the time.

Oddly enough, the school shared a name with the CIA's most notorious anti-communism crusade, The Phoenix Program. Sparked in 1967 as part of a reorganization of the war effort, the government of South Vietnam reincorporated all of its counterinsurgency activities into this program dubbed Phuong Hoang, a reference to a magical bird. In turn, their American counterparts adopted the name of the West's magical bird—the Phoenix.

The CIA Phoenix Program patch

That program's protocol was to round up, interrogate, and, sometimes, fatally torture regular South Vietnamese citizens—including the elderly—in an attempt to rout out any Viet Cong. In a war in which an enemy soldier could look exactly like a friendly villager, desperate measures were taken in an attempt to protect U.S. soldiers from hidden threats. These efforts, known as rural pacification, cost the lives of countless Vietnamese civilians, and one cannot help but conclude, the peace of mind and self-respect of the American soldiers who were, at times, forced into torture and murder.

At the time the little school in Saigon took its own magical-bird name, The Phoenix Program was probably

(left)

My brother John and I with our black poodle, Duffy, in the foyer of our Saigon home. You can see the plastic safety windows on the right.

a still well-kept secret but it's disconcerting to think that the educational institution I attended for most of my third-grade year shared a name with a systematic government control operation. That coincidence could very well be the reason that the board of directors planned to change the school name in time for the opening of the 1975-76 school year.

But of course, by that time, it no longer existed.

(right)

I am not quite sure why we have a 1975 envelope from Borgata Trigoria (Metropolitan City of Rome Capital) addressed to the CIA director William Colby in our family archives. I can only surmise that my father saw it on his desk at the CIA headquarters and asked if he could keep it for his stamp collection.

AUGUST 1974

August was a pivotal month politically for America but
a relatively quiet one for us. Life in Saigon was much
more confined than the wide open spaces of Taiwan,
but we were settling into routines. Though busy with
the pressures of the office, my father made as much time
as he could to spend with the reunited family. Stamp
collecting became a favored pastime. He spent hours
helping each of us pore over mail-order catalogs, discussing options, choosing favorite stamps, and filling
out order forms. It created a quiet, orderly atmosphere
in the cavernous house.

    In contrast, politics back home were in an unprece-
dented state of disarray. As of this writing, August 1974
holds the inauspicious honor of being the only month
in history in which a standing U.S. president left the

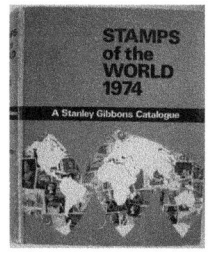

White House under threat of
impeachment. Richard Milhous
Nixon had been elected the 37th
president of the United States in
1968. He was a vicious politician as
well as a paranoid and quirky man.
He had every conversation in the
Oval Office recorded, a practice
which proved fatal to his defense

against charges that he colluded in the Watergate scandal. His tapes were subpoenaed by the Supreme Court and, when released on August 5, provided compelling evidence of Nixon's complicity in covering up a June 1972 break-in to the Democratic National Committee headquarters by Republicans. With the certainty of impeachment by the Senate on charges of obstruction of justice, abuse of power, criminal cover-up as well as several violations of the Constitution, Nixon announced his resignation, effective at noon on August 9, 1974.

It seems so black and white now.

Back then, it wasn't.

For or against Nixon, it was unsettling for the nation. My mother was sick at heart.

"Well, it looks as though Nixon has had it," she wrote to her parents. "Even if he is wrong, it still makes one want to weep. Ah well . . . what is there to say."

While American televisions were tuned to the Watergate trials and Nixon's resignation, the unsuccessful cease-fire was continuing in South Vietnam, creating floods of refugees—many of them orphans—into urban centers across the country. Artillery fire could be heard

THE WHITE HOUSE
WASHINGTON

August 9, 1974

Dear Mr. Secretary:

I hereby resign the Office of President of the United States.

Sincerely,

Richard Nixon

The Honorable Henry A. Kissinger
The Secretary of State
Washington, D.C. 20520

The President's resignation letter is addressed to the Secretary of State, in keeping with a law passed by Congress in 1792. The letter became effective when Secretary of State Henry Kissinger initialed it at 11:35 a.m on August 9, 1974.

(left)

It takes a certain level of personal egotism to hold public office. Nixon paraded his brash confidence by flashing his signature "Vs" on the campaign trail and at presidential public appearances.

from Saigon, rounds of 155s into Viet-Cong-held terri-tory just a hair's breadth from our home in the city.

Jimmy said one of his only memories of being six in Saigon was of watching rosy bursts of artillery from the roof of our house of an evening.

"I didn't know what it was," he said. "But I didn't think it was good."

"The peace and ceasefire in Vietnam are curious," wrote my father to his sister in August. "Da Nang is hit with five dead yesterday and the general level of fighting kicked off by the North Vietnamese is rising daily. Most people may be thinking of Watergate, Nixon, inflation, and gas prices, but war is very close and very real to us here."

The South Vietnamese were particularly vulnerable to the outcome of the political turmoil in Washington. It wasn't just a philosophical matter of who was going to take office but what policies the new president was going to adhere to in light of the Vietnam question; the slightest change in the winds could spell disaster.

Despite the mounting evidence to the contrary, my father was holding onto his conviction that his efforts would be successful. "Sometimes the best moments are the darkest ones, as Churchill told us. I still have faith that we will win."

My father's optimism, in retrospect, was not well-placed, nor broadly felt among the South Vietnamese populace. Nixon's resignation initiated its own domino effect that would not stop until the Americans were run out of Saigon. The citizens of South Vietnam seemed to know this instinctively. Within hours of Nixon's resignation, rumors of an ill omen put Saigon on the sweat: A boulder sitting atop a hill above President Thieu's native village had inexplicably cracked in two. Soothsayers could not help but cast the incident in a dark pallor, a foreshadowing that the worst yet was to come.

Oblivious to such signs, the whitewash of American politics rolled on. Gerald Rudolph Ford, sworn in on August 9, 1974, concurrently with Nixon's resignation, immediately expressed the intention to carry out the policy of his predecessors in regards to South Vietnam. He sent a letter to South Vietnamese President Nguyen Van Thieu on August 10, reassuring him of continued support. Thieu proudly read the letter to his cabinet.

"They thought that, well, even if Mr. Nixon had resigned, they can still believe in a commitment from the U.S. to help South Vietnam," Bui Diem, the Vietnamese Ambassador-at-Large said later.

What they didn't know, however, was that President Ford had sent letters to several allies on that same day, assuring *all* of them of the same continued support. But these were just letters, not an act of Congress.

Before long, senior congressional leaders would inform Ford and his Secretary of State Kissinger that Vietnam was just one of many urgent issues. The oil crisis and a struggling domestic economy loomed larger than the needs of a flagging Asian army half a world away, especially one in a country that had caused so many Americans such dissension and heartache.

With so many congressmen facing re-election pressures, the unpopular and divisive subject of Vietnam was not going to be brought up willingly, if at all. That message was not relayed to Thieu and his cabinet; they were allowed to believe that the fate of Vietnam was still dear to the American heart.

While these issues were pressing in on the powers-that-be, we as a family simply carried on, settling into our new life in Saigon. Home renovations were continuing; we finally had lights and air-conditioning on all three floors, a working telephone, and a bona fide (if tiny) swimming pool at the center of the house.

One thing that we still didn't have was a washer and dryer. "It makes me sick," my mother wrote, "The maids sit and scrub the clothes on the tile floor. They are the clothes-destroyers in action . . ."

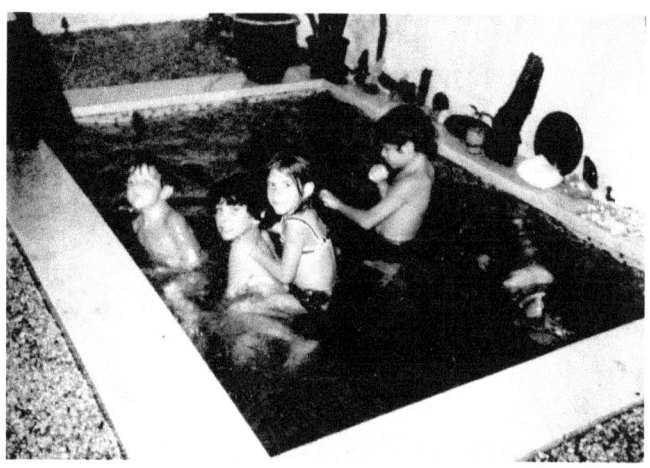

March 4, 2013

I remember the big housewarming party my parents had at the
end of August in 1974. But only very little. Much the shame,
for it was the event of the month in Saigon, inspiring even the
biggest bigwig of the South Vietnamese army, General Tran
Van Trung to attend. He arrived in two cars—the only cars
allowed into our little alley. Everyone else had to find parking
on the city streets and make their way through the mud from a
recent rainstorm to our front door. They also walked under the
inspection of armed guards who were stationed for three blocks
around our house!

I don't recall the pomp and circumstance of the General's
arrival, though I am sure there must have been a great deal. Our
front yard—which was essentially a "lawn" of small opaque
white pebbles about the size of a parking place—had been con-
verted into the guard tower location. Built of metal sheeting
for sides and roof, it served before and after the party as quite
a nice playhouse for tea parties and such. But of course, during
the party, the armed guards needed the space for guarding the
important military guests. I regarded them suspiciously with
their gray uniforms and large guns. They seemed, I thought,
out of place in my playhouse, but since I had no choice about
their being there, I made no fuss.

Instead, I found my way in and out of the crowd that had
suddenly taken over our space, our three-story house in this
new city that I knew so little about. My mother and father
circulated about, guiding people to eat at the buffet downstairs

and up to the roof for music and dancing. My dad worked at a radio station and knew a lot of musicians so we had the best bands in the country there. They played under the canopy of a real parachute that had perhaps, I liked to think, carried some young soldier to safety.

My favorite part of the evening came when my dad pulled me from the shadows to dance with him. I was clumsy at it and he told me to step onto his feet. His leather shoes were a perfect stoop for my little sandaled ones and we twirled around the dance floor as if on wings.

He looked down on me with a big grin on his face and, at that moment, I knew I was his favorite person at the party. Not the intimidating generals, not the famous singers, not the hundreds of friends and neighbors nor even the siblings whose size and demeanors often overshadowed my own quiet ways. It was me, there on the rooftop, floating on his footsteps, safe in his grasp.

Well, we had our big housewarming party for VietNamese and American friends and it was a huge success to say the least. But, what a job and Jim and I were both so happy when it was all over. About 2 hours before it was to begin a big storm hit and the rain poured down for about an hour. We all tore to the roof and grabbed the flowers and table cloths off of the 10 tables set up and got the band's instruments inside. But, fortunately, the rain stopped and we were able to set it all up again before the guests arrived. About 100 people came and on the roof we had a band and good singers - professional - from downtown. (Jim was able to get them to come in as they sometimes do work for him at his studio.) The buffet was set up in the dining room so I had a job of circulating from top to bottom getting people to eat...rather than just dancing. The whole affair was really funny tho - - as General Trung was attending, - - for 3 blocks around our house there were security guards and his car and our chief's car were the only two allowed to drive into our alley. Everybody else had to park elsewhere and walk back and up our very muddy alley due to the rain. Anyway, all of the work and strain was worth it as a good time was had by all - - and our kids and some of their friends really had a ball too. (If I ever do anything that large again I think I'd just have a cocktail party... the big job seemed to be the 100 plates, 100 sets of knives, forks and spoons, 100 wine glasses and 100 coffee cups...... fortunately this house could handle that number with the roof garden.)

Nancy Welch's letter home describing the Saigon housewarming party of the year, 1974.

SEPTEMBER 1974

On a hot clear Sunday early in September 1974, my mother took the older siblings—Michelle, Chris, Mike, and John—on a city walk to tour the ships docked along the Saigon River, enjoy a Coke on the terrace of the Continental Hotel (where author Graham Greene penned much of his book *The Quiet American),* and to enjoy the cool interior of the stately Notre Dame Cathedral. It was an enjoyable outing of several hours despite the heat but one, she feared, that would not be repeated. Americans didn't walk often in the city due to a "small element of fear" caused by rogue elements. One of these was the presence of moped robbers, or "cowboys," who would snatch purses, jewelry, or any other valuables an unsuspecting pedestrian might forget to hold close. Their strikes were most often simple hit-and-run thefts, with no intention of personal injury, but they could still be disconcerting.

Michelle had an up-close-and-personal encounter one day when she was on a shopping trip alone, before the awareness of the need for caution began to seriously limit our movements. She had stepped out of the American PX (the Army general store), and was about to get into a waiting cab, when a young man jumped off the back of a motorcycle, grabbed the paper bags from her arms and drove off.

(left)

Saigon's Hotel Continental was renamed the Continental Palace during the war and became well-used by foreign correspondents.

(top)

The hotel served as both a place to write and a setting for English author and journalist Graham Greene's 1955 novel The Quiet American.

"I didn't even have a second to think, or to be startled," she said. "He didn't threaten me or anything, he just wanted my groceries."

She turned to the cab driver, "Let's get him, let's go."

The driver barely looked at her and just shook his head. He wasn't going to go up against any Saigon cowboys, no way. And that was that.

Though we were ultimately never victims, the threat infiltrated our daily lives. One day, when we were expecting company, my mother put on a heavy gold chain that hung like a small rope down her fashionable silk shirt. I admired it, reaching out one small finger to touch its glittering weight.

"I'd never wear this out on the streets," she said. "If one of those cowboys drove by on his moped and grabbed it, it would rip one's head right off."

I tried not to think about that and filed it away with other untenable ideas, like the possibility of being shot after curfew or peppered by bombs.

Fortunately at the time, I didn't see the letter she wrote home about that walk, which concluded with an additional description of why walking tours were not to be *de rigueur*. "It is also a known fact that VC are in the city and people periodically do burn themselves up. We are always to avoid any large crowd of people milling about. So riding seems to be the order of the day. Such a shame."

Her reference to people who "do burn themselves up," is curious as there are no recorded incidents of self-immolation in the '70s, though it was carried on as a political act throughout the sixties. The most notable incident was on June 11, 1963, when Buddhist monk Thich Quang Duc had his body set aflame on a crowded Saigon street.

When I began to study the Vietnam Era, I initially assumed that the monk was protesting U.S. military build-up in Vietnam, just as Americans were beginning to do in the States. I was shocked to realize, then, that the reason this devout monk, whose religion included reverence for all life—including, one must suppose, his own—set himself on fire was not to call attention to the fighting between the North and the South, but to the mistreatment of the Buddhists by the government that we, the United States of America, were supporting!

Quang Duc was protesting the autocratic rule of South Vietnamese President Ngo Dinh Diem. His last words, which he wrote down for publication after his death, were a "respectful" plea to Diem to choose "clarity and compassion" for all religions. No response was forthcoming and four more monks and a nun used the same tactic before Diem was finally killed by his own generals in a coup in November of that year.

Quang Duc's sacrifice was photographed by Malcolm Browne, who won a Pulitzer Prize for it, and that single image is credited as the "match" that struck a flame to the question of Vietnam around the world, and was perhaps even the catalyst that cemented the American public's interest in helping the far-off country.

"No news picture in history," said John F. Kennedy, "has generated so much emotion around the world as that one."

Again, ironically, it is worth noting that he was protesting the government we were supporting. When another American-supported leader, *Nguyen Van Thieu*, took power in 1963, his human-rights policies were not much better. In fact, we supported him because he was *not* a communist more than any other factor. He did not believe in religious or intellectual freedom any more than the communists, and continued the persecution of the Buddhists.

Fortunately, we never ran into any burning bodies in the streets. The Viet Cong, however, were another story. While I don't recall any direct contact, there was the sense that they were always there, ever present. The "VC in the city" were part of a loosely organized, yet firmly committed, communist guerrilla network. The term "VC" or "Viet Cong" is a disrespectful contraction of Vietnam Cong San or Vietnamese Communists.

The American political and military agenda stemmed from a communist vs. non-communist world view, but the Vietnamese did not come from a tradition of distinct social and governmental building blocks in the same way that Western countries operate. Their long national heritage was one of a system of life that was based on the close-knit structure of familiarity: family, village, community. Therefore, any interloper was a threat, no matter the philosophy behind the intrusion.

The U.S., with its ideology of anti-Communism, meant nothing to the Vietnamese people in general and the Viet Cong were acting not for communism or against democracy, but for Vietnam and their right to self-rule.

It is no small coincidence that this impulse is an echo of the calls for independence that informed the very beginnings of our country. The North Vietnamese leader, Ho Chi Minh (literally the Bringer of Light), had no greater desire than to create an independent Vietnam. He chose his words carefully when, on September 2, 1945, in front of a crowd of hundreds of thousands of Vietnamese, he declared Vietnam an autonomous nation, free from foreign rule. The United States had been supporting him and his troop of fighters, the Vietminh, during World War II, against the Japanese incursion into their country, and he wanted to both thank America, and to make an appeal for further support. He began his speech boldly:

> "All men are created equal. The Creator has given us certain inviolable Rights; the right to Life, the right to be Free, and the right to achieve Happiness."

In a "quiet and clear, warm and friendly" voice he continued, giving clear attribution to Thomas Jefferson and the founding principles of the U.S.:

> "These immortal statements are taken from the Declaration of Independence of the United States of

America in 1776. In a larger sense, this means: All the people on the earth are born equal, all the people have a right to live, to be happy and free."

Ho subsequently wrote to President Harry S. Truman, requesting support for their fight for independence against France, which had been colonizing Vietnam since the mid-1800s. But France was a long-time ally of America. Additionally, Ho Chi Minh had long since adopted the communist philosophy as his conduit for "life, liberty and the pursuit of happiness," an approach that Truman could not synthesize into his world-view. Therefore, he simply did not respond and Ho Chi Minh felt he had no choice but to turn to Communist China

and the Soviet Union for support. While his fundamental philosophy was vastly different from the two traditionally communist governments, the liaisons cemented the image that the North Vietnamese politicians were cut from the same totalitarian cloth as the two superpowers, paving the way for the war against them.

But, of course, in 1974, as a family welcomed into the "safe" city of Saigon, we only knew the Vietnamese communists and Viet Cong as a bewildering threat to our lives and livelihoods. Over the coming months we would become more familiar with their presence than we ever cared to be.

Another fun family activity was visiting the Zoo. As my mother wrote home on September 30, "I took the kids and a couple of others to the Zoo not long ago and it was such a pleasant surprise. It is a much larger and prettier Zoo than the one in Taipei or Korea. The animals were very clean and the grounds are spacious . . ."

OCTOBER 1974

South Vietnam doesn't have four seasons, it has two: very hot and rainy, and hot and dry. As the rainy season came to a close in October 1974 and the weather cooled slightly, the intensity of the "war in peace" picked up. Congress had confirmed only $700 million in support for the fiscal year ahead which sentenced the ARVN to desperate half measures in their attempts to defend against the escalation by Northern forces.

Additionally, the Southern army was suffering under the disadvantage of the corruption of its own leadership. The situation under President Thieu's administration became so dysfunctional that its effects reached right down to the infantrymen. Often the South Vietnamese troops were unable to feed their families and morale was suffering greatly. Due to the exploitation of the ever-dwindling resources by the officers even artillery support sometimes had to be paid for.

"As long as security was good and living standards decent, the people tolerated corruption and inefficiency in government," South Vietnamese politician *Nguyen Ngoc Huy* said. "These defects are becoming less and less tolerable as security and living standards decline and numerous large-scale scandals bring into the open the rotten character of the leaders of the regime. If Thieu continues to govern with the support of corrupt and incompetent men while rejecting any true dialogue with other non-Communists, it will be difficult for South Vietnam to win the struggle against the Communists, whether it is fought militarily or politically."

The political situation did take a sudden and unexpected turn. On October 8, the North announced its refusal to deal with Theiu. They demanded a new leader if there were going to be any further talks about a negotiated settlement in which North and South could share a government.

President Thieu responded by firing four members of his cabinet, demoting nearly 400 field-grade officers, and removing three of his four regional commanders. His conciliatory attitude didn't last long, however, as he quickly did an about-face and slapped new controls on the press and warned opposition groups that they continued to agitate at their peril.

His methods backfired when, on the afternoon of October 10th, thousands of people took to the streets, surging past police lines to join the hundreds of journalists who were demonstrating against the government's repressive new laws.

Upon observing the sight of so many people agitated enough to protest, one Western journalist commented, "Thieu's really in trouble, I didn't believe it before, but I believe it now."

◆ ◆ ◆

The pressure on my father in this situation was rugged, and he came home daily visibly worn by the weight of his task to portray the South as a desirable place to defect to. My mother wished that she could send him away to relax, but there was no safe place to go.

"The situation here is not the best," she wrote home at the end of the month. "If the VC keeps blowing up the bridges soon we won't be able to get out of the city at all. There are several cities one could visit in a day and I'd sure like to go....but one always has the fear that the VC might be in the area and they really seem to be."

While my parents may have tried to keep the unrest in the city at an arm's length—just something they read about in the papers and avoided by never walking on the city streets—it became very real to us in two ways.

The first was that our cook, *Hoa*, was beside herself about the plight of her teenage son, *Amin*. He had just finished military school and was due to be deployed any day. Five of Amin's friends had gone into battle weeks before and only two returned. Hoa had already lost his father, a French man, to the VC nine years earlier.

"He is such a nice 18-year-old boy," my mother wrote home, "and actually looks just like an American kid. At any rate, Pleiku seems to be certain death and we are all dismayed. Hoa said if she pays the big whips 200,000 Piasters (about $330) he can be assigned to the Saigon area but she would have to sell her house to do it."

My mother said that they were toying with the idea of loaning her the money, but that Amin could still be killed in the battles around Saigon, though it was less likely. "So, we are going through a crisis of conscience. I don't really believe in buying people off, but it is a way of life here. If one has the money they don't have to fight."

Amin survived the worst of the fighting and was included in my father's list of those he would escort out of the country. Hoa declined the invitation for her family, but later fled the country on a small boat, though we never heard from her again.

◆ ◆ ◆

The second way that the unrest affected us was that on October 31, another anti-Thieu protest ruined our Halloween. It started out as a normal Thursday, even if we were a little bit hyper at the thought of going to the Embassy that evening for a party and lots of candy. As we sat in our classrooms in the Phoenix Study Group site at 192-194 Cong Ly Street, we were unaware of the flurry of activity in the school office down the hall.

"We're shutting down the school," the secretary said when she got my mother on the phone. "Send your driver to get your kids home."

She didn't wait for a reply but clicked right through to another call; there were nearly 100 families to reach and time was short.

Our driver, Mr. Bi, had to argue with the police to get past the barbed wire they had set up to keep the protesters out of the main city streets. After much yelling, the officers finally let him through. He crept along and finally entered the gates of the school in line with the other cars sent to pick up school children. The demonstration would make American headlines, the Oxnard Press-Courier in California proclaiming that "Riot Police Battle Thieu Protesters; Violence Paralyzes Saigon."

I remember the confusion of that morning, the way one remembers a bad dream. There had been one day earlier in the year when I had thought I'd been

forgotten at the school; I'd mixed up the pickup time, thinking it was noon and not 12:30 p.m.. As I'd watched the minute hand creep along on that day, the worry I'd been left behind seeped through me like a slow poison.

But on the morning of Halloween, there was no time to watch the clock, we were rushed from the classrooms to our cars in a desperate attempt to get us home safely.

As Mr. Bi, our chauffeur, drove out of the school gates and through the throngs of people in the streets, I peered out at a dangerous city. Struck dumb by the incomprehensible roar of discord, I was slowly

As smoke billows from a burning motorcycle, South Vietnamese riot police face several thousand angry protesters who sought to move their anti-corruption demonstration from suburban Saigon to the center of the city on Oct. 31, 1974. Authorities contained the crowd.

85

beginning to realize that my understanding of the world was in shambles.

That night, in an almost comical attempt to rescue the holiday, my parents felt the need to provide a veritable house of horrors, though I am sure I had had enough for one day. My mother sat all of us down in the living room, except for Michelle who was upstairs hiding with my father. Chris, Mike, John, Jimmy, Kim, and myself were sent upstairs one-by-one into sheet-draped bedrooms, veritable caverns of darkness to "trick-or-treat."

"They had fun as we scared the 'H' out of them," my mother wrote.

NOVEMBER 1974

In late November, my mother was contemplating how
bad the Vietnam situation seemed when my father suggested a short road trip.

"We should all go visit Bien Hoa soon," he said one
afternoon over martinis. "It's just a short drive, 15 miles
or so."

"Why's that?" my mother asked.

"Well, we'd better go before we can't go anymore," he
replied simply.

Bien Hoa was home to one of the largest military
bases in South Vietnam and had been a primary target
in the 1968 Tet Offensive, a climactic attack on American and South Vietnamese forces by the Viet Cong. As
a strategic holding, it was a regular target for military
skirmishes and if the "uneasy peace" continued to
escalate, it would certainly be closed for business sooner
than later. However, it wasn't the airfield my father
wanted to visit but the town, for sightseeing, lunch, and
some shopping, perhaps.

Plans were made for the following week. The day
before, though, my mother had second thoughts—what
if it was "Get Americans Day" in the little town? She
had just learned from another CIA wife that there was

a random, but persistent, Viet Cong system of establishing such times.

"But this seems to be a city of rumors," she wrote home, "one does not know what to believe."

Instead of going to Bien Hoa, she planned another trip to Vung Tau, the favorite beach spot for Embassy families in 1974-75 and for military personnel before the cease-fire. It was indeed a beautiful spot and holds a favorite place in my heart as one of the wide open spaces that seemed as safe as any place I'd ever been. Michelle, however, tells a different story.

She and another 15-year-old friend were enjoying the chance to roam, and had taken off alone down the wide, silvery beach. Thinking they might explore the cool shade of the trees bordering the sand, they headed toward them. Just then a soldier appeared out of the dark shadows.

"Unh! Unh! Unh!" he exclaimed gutturally. "Unh! Unh! Unh!"

Michelle and her friend froze in their tracks and the man in uniform repeated his intense barks.

"Unh! Unh! Unh!" He shook his gun at them in tempo with his grunts. He shot out a warning in words

The VN situation really does not sound good - - but this seems to be a city of rumors and one does not know what to believe. If one wants to go to a place on town one day... someone says.... that is a day to stay home as it is "get Americans day". Today Jim said we should go out to Ben Hoa! (15 miles) I said why. He said we had better go before we can't go anymore. Ah yes, how encouraging! So

they could not understand, but they got his meaning: "Do not come into this forest, little girls. DO NOT!"

My sister said that after that, beach visits were never quite the same. In fact, nothing in South Vietnam was ever to be quite the same again after November 1974, though no one at the Embassy could get past their presuppositions enough to see the writing on the wall. A great deal of intelligence was being received indicating communist troop movement, but while the information about the North Vietnamese preparing an offensive was endlessly pored over, the analysts and leaders could not come to an agreement about what it meant.

On the Washington front, Kissinger raised the issue of Vietnam in meetings with both China and the Soviet

The four Welch brothers (l-r, Jimmy, Chris, Mike, and John) on the beach at *Vung Tau*. About 60 miles south of Saigon, it was one of our favorite recreational destinations. My mother said it was "always a wonderful place to go to get out of the city and breathe the sea air." In April 1975 it would become a main evacuation site and quickly fall to the North Vietnamese Army.

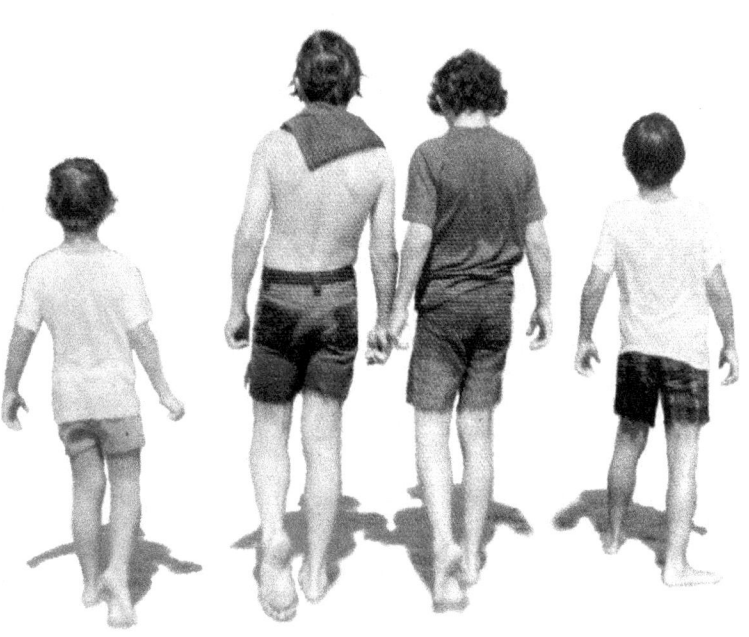

(left)

My mom wrote home to her parents in November 1974 explaining how travel was sometimes limited due to "get Americans day."

Union but the Communist superpowers had decided that the Saigon regime was doomed and were now preoccupied with their growing rivalry for increased influence in the region; they were not interested in discussing diplomatic solutions with the U.S.

Meanwhile, North Vietnamese reinforcements were quietly but quickly moving down their well-established trail systems, filing into position in the South. Their approach did not appear as methodical in the past but their fixation on taking Saigon as soon as possible had propelled them into high gear more quickly than anyone had anticipated. In contrast to their usual meticulous methods of preparing for an offensive, they were losing no time; they were certainly intent on their goal, not just to "get Americans," but to get Americans completely out of Vietnam, once and for all.

... the boys are playing basketball and the last two Sundays have played against Chinese teams from Cholon. We lost both games but our team consists of a few that want to play and the kids meet with their "coach" twice a week for organized practice. Chris played almost the whole game and did very well—it is his best sport. If you think I got excited during the baseball games—you should see me during the basketball games.

– Mother's Letter Home, October 25, 1974

The beat goes on with basketball games each Sunday. The 10-speed bikes are fixed now so Chris and Mike ride to and from school at times and also out to the Defense Attache's Office (DAO) where the basketball gym is. All of the kids ride here but the traffic is wild and unpredictable.

– Mother's Letter Home, November 22, 1974

A banner from the American basketball team in Saigon. According to player Fred C. Thomas, "Most of the boys attended Phoenix Study Group. This is a memento we would give to the Vietnamese teams we played.

Chris is really playing good basketball now—they finally won a game and lost on Sunday by one point. Mike does well too, but his best sport is baseball which he misses. John is now on a basketball team too.

– Mother's Letter Home, February 4, 1975

The boys are still furiously playing basketball every day. Hopefully this weekend they will have a couple of games against the Chinese.

Mike had the stitches [from appendix operation] out last Friday but feels good and is chomping at the bit to get back to basketball. It was a blow for his basketball team as he is the best player.

Chris is really some basketball player—he is a wee bit taller than me now and has a great body build. I guess I should say— Chris was a great basketball player as he is now out of action for a while too. Tuesday I went to watch the kids practice—as exciting as a real game—Phil went up to lay in a basket and Chris went up to try to block him and they were both going hard. Suddenly two boys were rolling all over the floor. Evidently as Phil was coming down and Chris was going up Phil's elbow hit Chris in the eye. Phil thought he had broken his arm and Chris's eyebrow was laid wide open and another place was open on the lid.

I was relieved to see only *that* damage once we could stop the blood. I thought that the eye had been damaged. So, back I went to the emergency room at the hospital where they put seven stitches on his lid and eyebrow. Saturday we go back to check his eye and maybe remove the stitches but he won't be able to play in the game on Saturday and he's on the main string.

Our teams have been invited to go to Bangkok for a meet with the International School Bangkok team in April and we are trying to raise some money for them. We are having bake sales this weekend and the next and hope to get some pledges or donations from the business community. It is time they realize that we have a "going" American school here.

– Mother's Letter Home, February 24, 1975

DECEMBER 1974

Despite all evidence to the contrary, my parents doggedly kept things as normal as possible. In early December, they were planning a family trip to Thailand for Christmas, still hoping for a washer and dryer, and making time for unique Saigon experiences. One Friday, my father took the afternoon off of work, despite his pressing workload, and all nine of us boarded a small charter boat to take us on a cruise along the Saigon River for several hours.

Though it was a "wonderful, relaxing day" complete with a picnic lunch, reading, and an opportunity to

take steering lessons from our young South Vietnamese tour guides, we could not keep thoughts of war completely at bay. The sun was beginning to sink toward the horizon when Chris pointed toward the green-swathed shore dotted with low-lying buildings.

"There could be Viet Cong anywhere over there," he said to me.

I pursed my lips. I could imagine that there might be danger where he pointed but my eight-year-old brain could not fathom exactly what that might mean. What did a Viet Cong look like? Would I know one when I saw it? What would it do to me? I stared hard at the trees and bushes, wishing I could diminish the invisible threat by making it miraculously appear.

◆ ◆ ◆

Unfortunately, my wish was about to come true—or quite nearly true. We didn't get to see any identifiable Viet Cong, but began to feel their presence at uncomfortably close range. For one, we were informed that a South Vietnamese employee at House Seven—a typesetter—had been arrested due to suspicious activity. When interrogated, he confessed to being a Viet Cong infiltrator, a spy for the National Liberation Front.

My father's company car was immediately switched out and we had the plates changed on the family station wagon, but that hardly made us safe again.

House Seven was a close-knit group of people who spoke freely among themselves and came and went

My little brother Jimmy gleefully takes the helm on an afternoon river cruise on the Saigon River.

95

as they pleased. The two-story building was actually an old warehouse, its shabbiness meant to disguise its top-secret PSYOP mission. It was not even heavily guarded, another attempt to keep it under the radar. As an insider, the VC spy had access to much information about every American working at the station, including our house address.

"Obviously we can't move," my mother wrote in a half-hearted attempt to soothe her parents. "The VC probably knew where we lived before we moved in, anyway."

• • •

It soon became apparent that they did indeed know of our location. One day upon arriving at home from school, I heard an unusual noise coming from the second floor near my bedroom. I took the stairs two at a time, my little legs trembling with the effort. As I topped the last step, I realized that the noise was coming from my brother's room, which, though it was located right next to mine, had an outside entrance that could only be reached from the main house via a short balcony walk that overlooked our "little pool" in the central rock garden below and opened to the rooftop garden above.

As I stepped out onto the short balcony, the sound sheered out of the open door of his room. It was loud and grinding and not at all reassuring. I peered around the doorway to see my father, on his knees, pressing a smoking drill into the cement wall of my brother's bedroom. The perspiration dripping from his forehead startled me more than the noise. I don't think I had ever seen him sweat.

The white wall was strafed with gray gouges. They were wide but not very deep. Mr. Bi was looking on with studied intensity but even I could see the doubt in his face. John was watching with curiosity but not much conviction himself.

My father saw me and let the drill fall silent.

"Wh – what are you doing?" I asked.

"Trying to make a tunnel," Dad answered. "Your brother heard sounds on the balcony."

"Sounds?" I said.

"Your mother is afraid it might be the VC," he replied almost laconically. After all, what is one to do when living in such circumstances? He examined the torn-up bit, avoiding my eye. "She wants a way for John to be able to get to your room at night without going outside."

My heart lurched in my chest and a cold sweat pricked the nape of my neck.

Viet Cong in the center of our house? The enemy Viet Cong? Right next to where I slept? I was sorry I had ever wished to see them.

◆ ◆ ◆

It is worth repeating here that the Viet Cong were communists but they were distinct from the North

Vietnamese Army (NVA) which was an organized military similar to any other country's. The VC was the primary guerrilla force that occupied pockets of South Vietnam and were responsible for so much of the hardship that American soldiers endured—they operated in a coordinated but hardly traceable system, faded in and out of sight like ghosts, and blended in with the South Vietnamese villagers.

The NVA, by contrast, moved in battalions, directed by a Hanoi-based leadership. In December, they began in earnest to take over parcels of land in remote areas. These were not strategic or valuable sites, but they were tests. Would the U.S. retaliate? Would there be any pushback for their escalated breach of the Paris Peace Accords signed in January 1973? Communist Party First Secretary *Le Duan* was watching the American political scene carefully. It was not long before he made up his mind that the extended and messy congressional debate in Washington D.C. was dissolving any backbone America had had in regard to Vietnam. It was becoming clearer and clearer that they would not be pumping any more funds into supporting the South Vietnamese Army. Le Duan concluded that the odds were truly in favor of the North's plans for further military advances.

In the last week of December, the NVA made a move on Phuoc Long, a provincial capital 75 miles northeast of Saigon. This was a step-up from the previous "land grabs." From a military standpoint, it was not a great loss as the city was located too far from Saigon to

Despite the pressures of the war building, James and Nancy Welch enjoyed being in each other's company again.

be a strategic gain, but it was a devastating blow to the South Vietnamese government.

The AVRN held out for a week under heavy attack but by January 7, 1975, they lost control of the city. The fact that the United States did not respond at all was demoralizing to the South and was the crack of a starting gun for the North. Le Duan made a speech to his colleagues the day after the province was captured encouraging them to "create conditions for a general uprising in 1976 to liberate all of South Vietnam" or—if opportunities presented themselves earlier—perhaps even in 1975.

The loss of Phuoc Long, which inspired three days of mourning in Saigon, marked the true beginning of the end, though no one realized it at the time.

JANUARY 1975

While the Phuoc Long fight was being waged and lost, our family was still on vacation in Thailand, for that "much-needed" holiday at the sea's edge. The only near-death experiences there were when the older boys got to go parasailing and Mike descended too quickly and got dunked in the warm waters and Chris went too far, scraping the fluttering edges of the palm trees on descent.

Like a parasailer just skimming the trees, the U.S. Embassy in Saigon considered the loss of Phuoc Long to be a near miss and nothing of consequence. So it was that we were allowed to return to Saigon when our vacation ended in early January 1975. Ultimately, despite the heightened military action by the North, U.S. Ambassador Graham Martin wanted everyone, both in Vietnam and in D.C., to believe that things were not as bad as they seemed.

Conversely, CIA Station Chief Tom Polgar was beginning to send mixed messages to Washington that were couched in terms of Armageddon. Both "spins" were meant to convince policymakers that Vietnam was deserving of attention and support. One message was a reassurance that all was well while the other was a bugling call to immediate action. The emotionally laden but contradictory messages began to wear down any meager support that had been lingering. The Ford administration still publicly held to its position that America had a moral responsibility to South Vietnam, but Congress was questioning what a few hundred million dollars in funds could do in a vacuum when billions had not made a difference when Vietnam had been fully staffed by American forces.

The scales were beginning to fall from President Thieu's eyes: he could not ignore the fact that the capture of Phuoc Long had not inspired *any* U.S. response. Neither Martin's reassurances nor Polgar's dire warnings were gaining any traction where it counted, and he could not shake the feeling that there would be no return from the disintegrating path he found himself on.

Even those most strategically poised to bolster aid were unresponsive. On January 7th, shortly after the siege at Phuoc Long, Kissinger called an emergency meeting of his crisis management team. It was there that CIA Director William Colby reminded everyone that the National Intelligence Estimate had ruled out a general offensive in 1975 and therefore there was no further call to action. He would later admit that it was he who had set the upbeat tone of the military activity forecast.

"Yes," he said sadly, "I was responsible for the judgment that nothing significant would happen until 1976."

These mixed messages filtered down into our daily

lives. Upon returning from our holiday, we found out that two CIA men had been killed in Saigon, one by a mine in his house and another aboard a plane—way too close for comfort. We could not help but reflect that the VC knew where we lived. Pessimism was descending on the population of Saigon like a monsoon rain cloud, the years of lies and fabrications making it hard to see what was real, and to know what to believe. The streets were filling with refugees including many orphans, and food prices were skyrocketing. Desperation was beginning to tinge every aspect of daily life.

In the midst of all that, my mother clung to one bright development. "I am obviously optimistic. The PX just got in washers and dryers, and we bought a set today. I've had enough of these smelly mildewed clothes . . ."

FEBRUARY 1975

February brought the celebration of Tet, the
Vietnamese New Year. Traditionally, it provided one
of the few long breaks during the agricultural year
between the harvesting of the crops and the sowing
of the next ones. Essentially, for the Vietnamese, it
is a combination of the festivity and good times of
Christmas and New Year's Eve. Our family was drawn
into the celebrations when Hoa, the maids, and Mr. Bi
bought and cooked us a traditional Vietnamese dinner
at our house.

A typical Tet holiday
decoration: a banner
declaring *"Chúc
Mừng Năm Mới"* or
Best Wishes for the
New Year

Since 1968, the holiday had become inextricably
linked with the most dramatic turning point of the war.
Known as the Tet Offensive, the massive Viet Cong
attack effectively tipped the war in the North's favor
despite the fact that they sustained major losses and
were essentially crippled by the effort. It was the visual
footage of the Tet battles that soured the American
public's support of the troops in Vietnam—how, after
three years of fighting and hundreds of thousands of
troops, could the enemy still mount such an attack? The
images and echoes of it still hung in the air in 1974, a
dark underscore to an otherwise happy time.

"Tet is really upon us and we are all praying that it
will be a quiet one," wrote my mother, adding that she

hoped the war didn't flare up too badly. "I realize how bad it all sounds there—much worse than it seems here."

Despite her assurances, she went on to admit that the House Seven employees were not feeling safe and were, in fact, making dire plans to avoid the wrath of the communists should their offensive continue.

"Jim asked Mai Lan, the radio star, what her family plan would be if the Commies took over and they could not get out. She said, 'My father will shoot us and then commit suicide.' It just seems unreal. However, there is a plan to get certain people out if necessary. Anyway, Tet is a time of happiness for the New Year mixed with anxiety."

Ambassador Martin's official line of optimism was being passed on to the families in an effort to assuage any panic that might be taking root. "Our leader gave us a briefing the other day," she wrote in late February, "and I am still not quite sure of what he said but he doesn't see this country falling in the foreseeable future and 'we are as safe here or safer than any large city in the U.S.' So, don't worry!"

Such confusing messages were putting her on edge, but she tried valiantly to stay positive, describing a visit to an orphanage in Gia Ding for an afternoon Mass and an open house, but even in that she couldn't get away from the growing truth. "It is a beautiful area and so quiet and peaceful (by day). By night it is war."

The same conflicted messages were being agonized

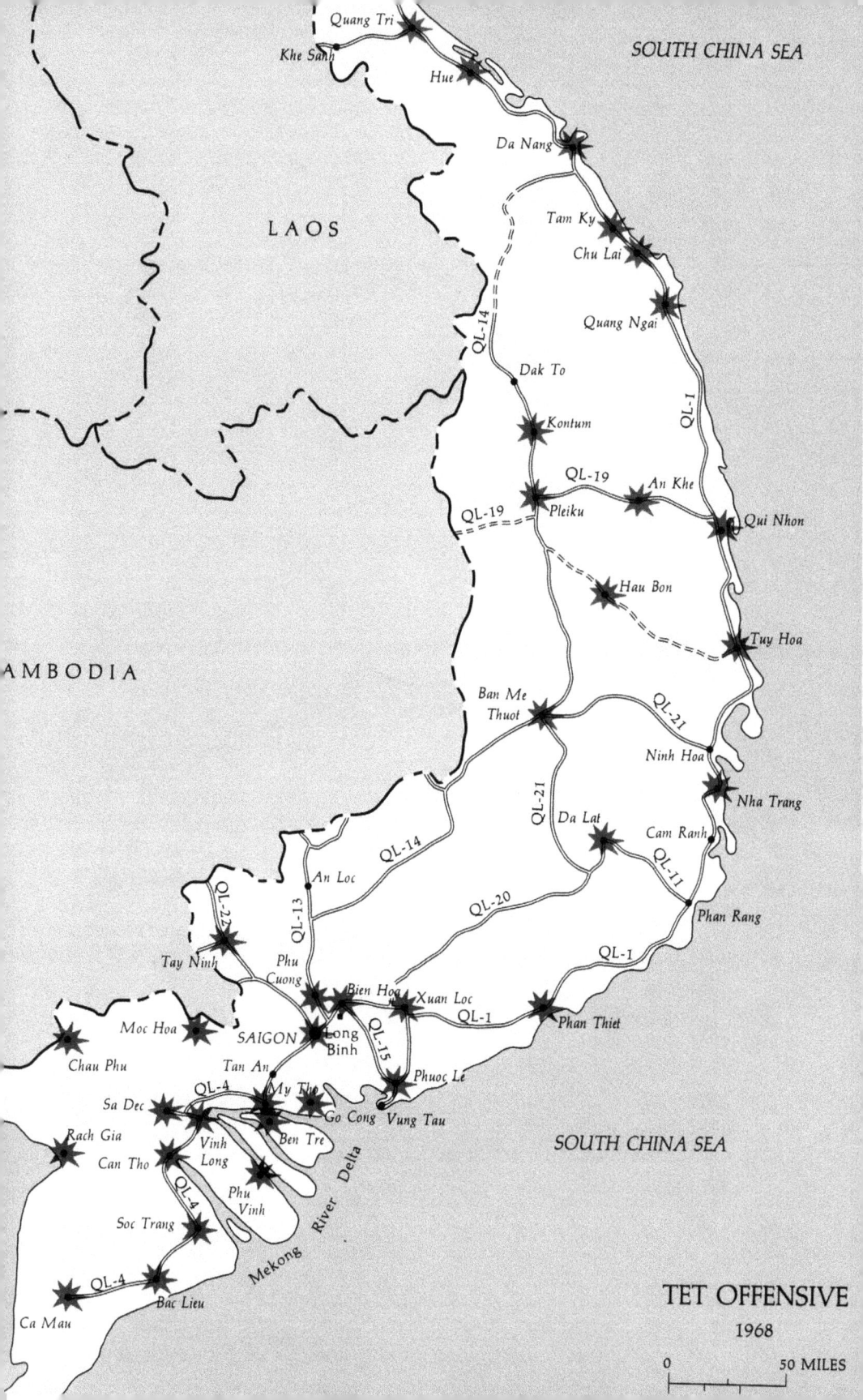

SOUTH CHINA SEA

Quang Tri
Khe Sanh
Hue

Da Nang

LAOS

Tam Ky
Chu Lai

Quang Ngai

QL-14

Dak To

Kontum

QL-19

An Khe

QL-19   Pleiku

Qui Nhon

QL-1

Hau Bon

Tuy Hoa

AMBODIA

Ban Me
Thuot

QL-21

Ninh Hoa

QL-21

Da Lat

Nha Trang

Cam Ranh

QL-14

QL-11

An Loc

QL-20

Phan Rang

QL-13

QL-22

Tay Ninh

QL-1

Phu
Cuong

Bien Hoa   Xuan Loc

QL-1

Phan Thiet

Moc Hoa

SAIGON   Long
Binh

QL-15

Chau Phu

Tan An

Phuoc Le

QL-4   My Tho

Sa Dec   Go Cong   Vung Tau

SOUTH CHINA SEA

Rach Gia

Vinh
Long

Ben Tre

Can Tho

Phu
Vinh

QL-4

Soc Trang

Mekong River Delta

QL-4

TET OFFENSIVE

Ca Mau   Bac Lieu

1968

0   50 MILES

over in Washington. Persistent requests for funding finally prompted select members of Congress to travel to Vietnam to see for themselves what was transpiring a half a world away. One of those inquirers was Representative Pete McCloskey of California, who immediately saw through the unsubstantiated messages of those on the ground in Saigon. After a visit in late February and early March of 1975, he was no clearer on how U.S. aid would benefit the turbulent situation.

"Graham Martin and his Station Chief [Polgar] were incapable of giving a fair appraisal to a visiting team of Congressmen," he said. "They were so emotionally wrapped up in the desire to save South Vietnam. Martin was saying the Vietnamese can stand, all you have to do is give them more ammunition and more equipment."

The delegation returned to the States unconvinced by this display of blind optimism and no further support was extended to the South Vietnamese Army. Meanwhile, the North Vietnamese were advancing their plans diligently, if carefully. Three divisions were deployed to surround the city of Ban Me Thuot in South Vietnam's Central Highlands. NVA artillery units shelled steadily for days so that the southern soldiers would not hear the tanks moving into place for a planned attack in early March.

My father was planning to take Chris, Mike, and John to Nha Trang for a few days to fish and snorkel "to their hearts' content." The resort town was just 115 miles

During the attacks, Saigon was overshadowed by thick black clouds of smoke. The attacks were unexpected because there was usually a tacit cease-fire during the festive holiday of Tet, the Vietnamese New Year.

southeast of the well-disguised military build-up taking place in Ban Me Thuot. Fortunately, their mid-February trip to the resort town was canceled due to logistical issues. A fellow CIA agent later reported that he and his son had visited Nha Trang just months earlier, when the fighting had been much quieter, only to narrowly miss being hit by a half-dozen Viet Cong B-40 rockets. One landed just 50 yards from them, leaving a hole a foot deep and two feet across.

My mother sent a copy of the school newsletter, The Dragon's Mouth, home in March of 1975, just three weeks before we were to flee. She encouraged her parents to read the publication and "notice super bowler John Welch in one picture. It is his favorite thing to do and for his birthday on Sunday we are giving him his own 10-pound gold bowling ball and carrying case."

MARCH 1975

On his birthday in mid-March, my brother John received a 10-pound caramel-swirl bowling ball. I stared at it, open-mouthed and incredulous. What luck, to own such a thing! He picked it up, demonstrating his ownership over it; it was not something to be shared.

He later confessed to me that he didn't think he was much good at the game, but I'll never forget the feeling of looking up to him as the one family member who deserved the honor of owning such a treasure.

Looking back, that gift, as much as anything else, depicts the ongoing denial of the time for—as anyone who's ever packed up household goods knows—you would never buy such a thing if you are anticipating a

Mr. Gene Westlake, checking scores.

BOWLING NEWS

A great deal of interest was ~ by students in organizing a bow league. Mr. Gene Westlake, a parent volunteer, came forward undertook the organizing, dire supervising and teaching of th

Every Saturday morning an enth group of about 59 youngsters ; in learning of the mastery of ~ ~ have been formed and

major move, much less a panicked evacuation, in the near future. As it was, we were just weeks away from my mother having to pack up 6,000 pounds of household goods into 24 boxes with barely any help or packing material.

On March 10th, six days before my brother's birthday, the NVA had descended on the idyllic village of *Ban Me Thuot*, just 150 miles north of Saigon, taking it in less than 30 hours. Initial reactions to the siege were muted. Kissinger, on a diplomatic mission en route from Cairo to Tel Aviv, was briefed by staffers. He looked surprised and puzzled for a moment but then simply shrugged and went back to his work at hand; he did not think the loss signified any real crisis.

In striking contrast, historian George J. Vieth begins his book, *Black April, the Fall of South Vietnam, 1973-75,* with a description of the battle of Ban Me Thuot and states, "Rarely in the history of nations can one point with such precision to the beginning of the country's demise."

The analyses are separated by some 30 years and with the benefit of hindsight. However, even at the time, the news shocked the Saigon community. In response to the reports brought home by my father on the 13th, my mother wrote, ". . . province officials were all captured and nine of the 12 were executed—by beheading! No bloodbath, indeed."

This written exclamation was the first indication that she was no longer falling prey to the official all-is-well

While recovering from having his appendix removed in early March, my brother shared his comic books with some South Vietnamese soldiers bunked near him. "Mike said that they like the war ones best – crazy!" wrote my mother.

line from the Embassy. For better or worse, she hardly had time to think about such things as she spent much of late February and early March at the hospital: Kim had a bad case of tonsillitis, Michelle was recovering from possible hepatitis, Chris's eyebrow had been split wide open on the basketball court, and Mike had emergency surgery for appendicitis.

Mike's recovery took place in a special medical ward usually reserved for Americans, but on this occasion it had been opened up to care for wounded South Vietnamese soldiers and thus his companions were six remaining members of an ARVN crew of 27 whose ship had been mined in the Mekong Delta. They knew little English but befriended my brother anyway, partly to

pass the time and partly to practice their English. Mike let them borrow his comic books, which they were only too happy about. Ironically, they liked the ones depicting battle scenes the best.

Meanwhile, my father took Jimmy to the Philippines to get a pair of much-needed eyeglasses. They rode in a military jet cargo plane that was not meant for shuttling humans and the two of them quite nearly froze to death during the flight. While he was gone, Michelle and my mother discovered that some of her extensive jewelry collection had gone missing, putting her in the awkward position of investigator, jury, and judge.

"I had to confront the three maids," she wrote, "and so had all kinds of weeping and wailing going on around here. It is their duty to watch the house so even if they didn't take it, they let someone else in here that did."

With the help of Mr. Bi they tried to find out what exactly had happened but there was no way, with the language gap, to pin down the facts and implications coupled with the extreme fear the maids were feeling about their future. Ultimately, she gave up trying to prove who had taken the jewelry and was utterly dismayed that the formerly close relationships were now overshadowed by regret and suspicion. Still, in the uncertain times, she did not feel that she could force them onto the street, that time seemed to be coming soon enough.

Such divides in communication and breaches of

trust had a long legacy in America's involvement in Vietnam and the worst was yet to come. The loss of Ban Me Thuot represented not so much the loss of one town, strategic though it was, but an irreversible rift in the South Vietnamese troops' trust in their leadership. They were left in the field with no clear direction or support. The corruption and dissolution of military command had reached such a level that the officers' every-man-for-himself attitude spread like wildfire, fanning rumors of defeat and inciting panic. Combatants' minds turned from their commitment to an ever-dwindling government ideal toward their own homes and families, many of which were located in the besieged areas. As news of the fall of that town spread, masses of civilians and soldiers alike rushed toward the coast in a desperate attempt to find safe haven, but there was none.

By late March, the North Vietnamese forces were closing in on the coastal city of Da Nang, where over 100,000 refugees were trying desperately to escape, some even handing family members, including small children, alone onto overloaded ships headed south. A World Airways jumbo jet landed in Da Nang to help with the situation. The plane was mobbed by a panicked crowd, and within ten minutes, three hundred Vietnamese, few of them women or children, had crammed themselves aboard. The plane took off, its rear stairway still lowered and covered with desperate men. As the aircraft gained altitude, those clinging to the edges of the open doorway fell to their deaths. It was this image—of the crush of humanity clamoring for safety—that would put the spurs on my father's impulse to get his South Vietnamese staff out of Saigon.

As late as March 27, nearly three weeks after the country began truly unraveling, my mother was still unsure if we would be able to get out. Unable to sleep and worried both about her overworked husband and her vulnerable children, she was surviving on nerves in the uneasy safety of the city.

"Such a soul-searching and nerve-wracking ordeal," she wrote to her parents. "We are all totally sick of heart. Saigon seems to be okay at the moment, but the situation is so precarious that we have requested (along with others with children) to be allowed to leave before our scheduled time in the summer."

Her request to depart became just one more piece of paperwork in the queue of pressing matters at the Embassy. With so many traumatic problems, the staff was overworked and overwhelmed to the point of distraction, my father included. It would not be easy to get permission.

One evening, my mother took a break from taping boxes to slam her hand on the dining room table while my father was going through the motions of fixing his routine martini. My father looked up, startled.

"We've got to get these kids out of here," my mother shrilled, the panic she'd been holding back suddenly bursting forth.

I saw my father smile wanly and regard my mother

with red and tired eyes. He shook his head slightly as if to dislodge cobwebs or exhaustion.

"I'll do what I can, Nance," he said. "Perhaps it's time."

"There had better be time," my mother snapped, stooping to strap another band of tape across the box at her feet. "There had better be time."

On the 29th of March, just four days before we would fly out, North Vietnamese forces captured Da Nang, sweeping across the vast air bases where U.S. forces had first been greeted with flowers in 1965.

Originally posted on March 10, 2019

Ah, a day at the beach with the kids. Sun, surf, severed heads in the sand.

Wait, what? This early-1970s photo shows five of the seven Welch kids happily ensconced in sand up to their necks. The caption scrawled on the back of the picture: "Shirley Faye did not like this picture. She said it 'looks like a war.'"

I don't remember that day at the beach but the reference to decapitation brought to mind my mother's letter of March 13, 1975:

> "We did get down to Vung Tau one Sunday–always a wonderful place to go to get out of the city and breathe the sea air . . . The children have nine days off for Easter vacation and I had hoped to go to Dalat and Nha Trang. However, I guess with the war situation as it is we'll just have to stay around Saigon . . . Jim received a report today from Ban Me Thuot and the province officials were all captured and 9 of the 12 were executed – – by beheading! No bloodbath, indeed."

My mother's friend did not like this picture of five of the Welch kids buried in the sand. I imagine it must have felt pretty good, but she said it "looks like a war.'"

APRIL 1975

A letter from our driver:

April 1st, 1975
Dear Sir and Madam,

Difficulty is coming ahead. We worry about the lot of the present situation of my country and think hard about our coming suffering days without jobs.

I know this sudden separation is beyond all of our will. I don't know what will happen to my family, then. Please, before leaving Saigon, do me a last favor—send me to or find me another job.

In my life, I do believe God will be with good and kind people like both of you, forever.

Hereby, I want to express my deepest heartfelt thanks for your immense kindness and your wonderful treatments toward me, so far.

Again, an oceanful of thanks.

Sincerely yours,
Bi

On the same day that Mr. Bi wrote this letter, CIA analyst Frank Snepp received intelligence from a highly reliable informant that Hanoi was indeed on a "blood scent," intent on a military takeover.

Meanwhile, my mother was scrambling with last-minute preparations. During those first days in April, she stacked the many boxes of household items to be—hopefully—picked up later by the shipping company. To be sure that nothing invaluable was lost, she mailed packages of family mementos, stamp collections, and clothes to her parents' house in Idaho.

She bought a new large purse that would accommodate the paperwork for the eight of us. As she was organizing it, Chris came downstairs with his fishing line and asked if she could carry it in her purse so that he and his Grandpa could fish once we arrived in Boise.

"Well, sweetheart, my purse will be so full of passports and shot records, I'm sure I won't have room for fishing line," she said. "Besides, I think Grandpa will have some there to fish with."

As Chris walked away, her heart felt heavy at the thought of all the small hopes and dreams that must die with an ending like this one. She felt almost ashamed to think of how much she had longed for a washer and dryer, when now so much more was at stake, especially for those they would be leaving behind.

When she let the two maids go, she gave them a cash bonus, despite the earlier incidents with the missing jewelry. The cook and the driver would stay on to take care of my father for as long as he remained, but she gave each of them jewelry they could sell; a pearl

In addition to caring for her big family, my mother often volunteered at orphanages, where she witnessed first hand the results of years of GI involvement with the local women. In one letter she wrote "It is really heartbreaking though to look at the kids; some of them have blond hair and scarcely a trace of Vietnamese can be seen in their faces."

necklace and gold chain for Hoa and a diamond ring to Mr. Bi. She would not be able to help Mr. Bi with his request about placing him in a new job, but she hoped that my father would be able to make something happen, perhaps even offering him a spot on his evacuation list.

Our original departure date was April 4th. We were to fly out with the initial Operation Babylift flight, a project launched by President Ford in an effort to save as many orphans, mostly Amerasian, as possible. Many of these children looked nearly completely Caucasian with blue eyes and blond hair. Left in Vietnam, they would meet with vicious treatment by the North Vietnamese who would see them as terrible reminders of the American presence in their country. The operation would eventually bring some 3,000 children to the United States.

My mother had volunteered to be one of the chaperones since she and Michelle had spent much time with orphans over the previous months. This flight was just one of many that was scheduled. Though the C-5A Galaxy transport was one of the largest planes available, it

with the aid from the Americans most of them seem to be in pretty good shape. It is really heart-breaking tho to look at the kids - - some of them have blond hair and scarcely a trace of Vietnamese can be seen in their faces. I am now the chairman to go to World Vision or Half Way House just to go out and help feed and change the babies and play with them. These little ones are all in the process of being adopted so just need some attention given to them - - they are basically healthy and just need to be fattened up before making the trip to the States - - I am also trying to get foster homes

became apparent that a family our size would be taking seats that the refugee children would otherwise have, so my mother changed our reservations to a commercial Pan Am flight departing the day before.

Our trip to the States, for various harrowing reasons, took two full days, and as soon as we landed, we heard of the fate of the first "too tragic" Operation Babylift plane. Shortly after takeoff, a warning light had come on and the pilot had attempted a wide turn to get back

to Tan Son Nhut. Before he could complete the return, the bottom of the airplane was torn apart by an explosion. The gaping hole immediately sucked the air from the cabin, instantly killing some of the 250 orphans and 50 volunteers abroad. Others were spewed into the air, still alive. Wildly out of control, the plane plummeted to the ground, careening nearly half a mile through the thick mud of the rice paddies. As it slid to a halt, water filled the cabin, drowning still more victims.

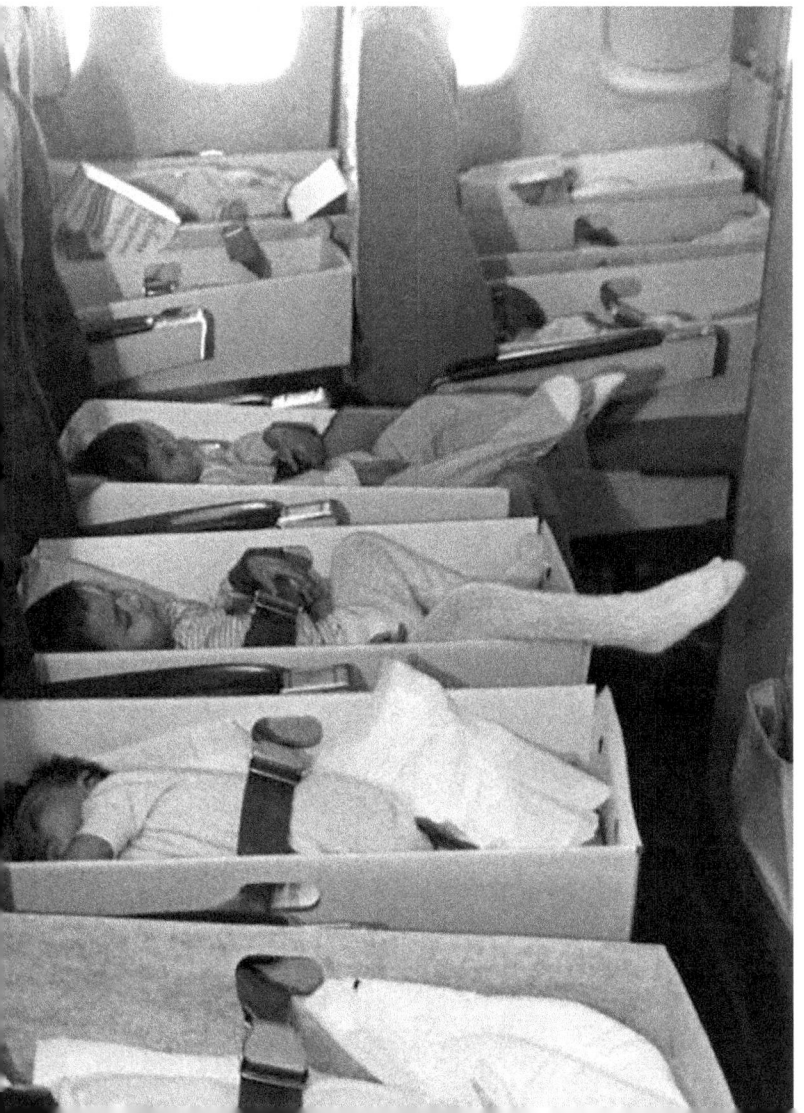

The tragedy struck those in Saigon like a blow to the heart. People flooded to the airport to lend a hand, to give blood, or to help unload the rescue helicopters that shuttled the injured from the crash site back to Tan Son Nhut.

"As the children were carried off the choppers, you couldn't tell if they were alive or dead. Nearly every one of them was covered from head to toe with mud . . . they were limp little rags," one rescue worker said.

At the time it was thought to be the second-worst crash in aviation history, taking more than 200 children and every adult but one. Later, it would be discovered that over half of the children did survive, but the losses were devastating nonetheless. My father wrote to my mother that night. He shared his anguish in five words: "What a tragedy! I cry."

Rumors quickly spread that the crash was caused by Viet Cong artillery fire, but the truth was much more unnerving: it was the result of a simple latch that had not been secured properly. In the stressful atmosphere that was Saigon in April '75, someone had failed to take the time to follow standard safety checks and it had reaped this disastrous result. What other tragedies might occur as the intensity of the evacuation picked up speed and the press of the enemy armies forced even greater panic?

And worse, how could those still in the country hold on to any hope when it felt as if the country was dying?

On March 27th, my mother wrote to her parents that ". . . we are all living on nerves, we may be coming but we are not sure so wait until you see the 'whites of my eyes!'"

A mere week later, on April 3rd, we took flight. A run-on excerpt from my mother's calendar tells about our "day:"

April 3 – April 4 – April 5
Chris to school to pick up records
Pearl and chain to Hoa (cook)
Diamond Ring to Mr. Bi (driver)
to airport 10:30
Mr. and Mrs. Tuan and Mai Lan to see us off
Bua with us
Ring and chain from Mrs. Tuan
Dep 782 Pan Am at 1:00 to Manilla
to Guam
left Guam
engine out
jettisoned fuel
back to Guam
wet down plane
to hotel arriving at 6
slept-in A.M.
stayed overnight again
dep for Hawaii
boarded same plane
at 12:30 engine out

to Hawaii to sleep 1½ hours
United 747 to S.F.
arrive – 5:30 cold
United to Boise arrive 9:00 p.m. 32°
weary

The next day we slept late, ate at McDonald's for the first time
in years, and went out to buy coats so we wouldn't freeze to
death in the Idaho spring weather.

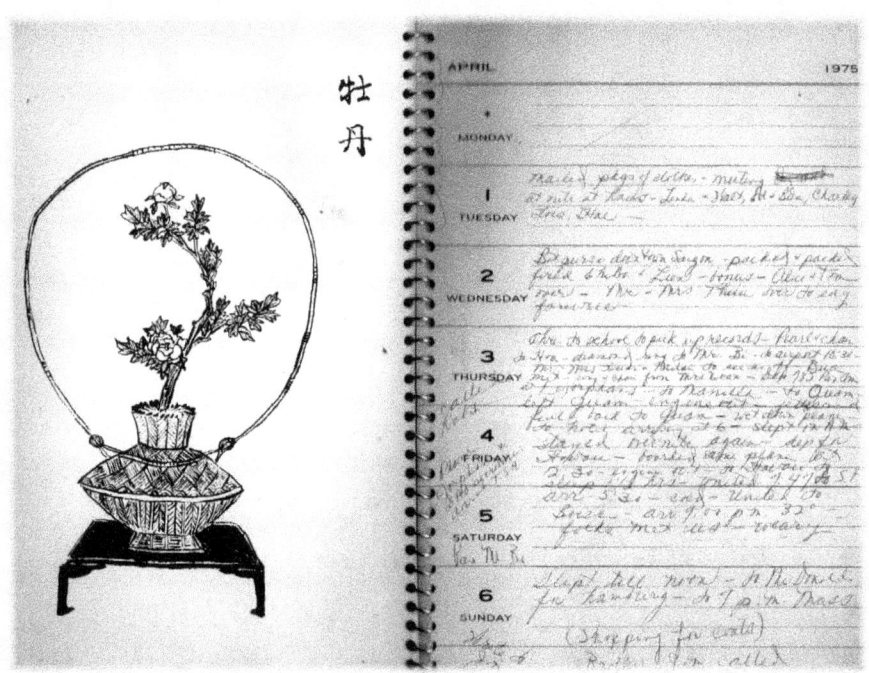

The two older boys—Chris and Mike—wrote to my father on April 6, 1975. They would not hear back from my father for nearly two weeks. On April 21st he wrote home that he had received all my mother's letters but had destroyed them, perhaps because they contained sensitive information. So was this letter spared because it was from his sons? Or did my mother hold onto it, never sending it when she knew it may not be received or could be destroyed?

Dear Dad,

We had a real hard trip and had to stay in Guam and Honolulu because the #1 engine broke down. Sorry I didn't get a postcard in Hawaii but I send all my love in this letter. Now we're in Boise, it's snowing, it just started tonight. Today it was 33°, ice cold. When we got here we didn't have any clothes so we froze. It's so nice to be back to the U.S. but it would be nicer if you were here. I hope the days go fast. Ya know what today we went to McDonald's. It was pretty good. We also went downtown and looked for clothes, most of us got coats, but I didn't get one. It seems like it changed here but I can't wait to see Virginia. Oh ya, Grampa said it's too cold to fish. I love and hope to see you soon. Goodbye with love.

Love, Your Son,
Mike [age 12]

Hi dad,

How have you been? Fine, I hope because I want to see you soon. I have been wondering when you are going to get home? Is it sometime in early June, [that] is supposed to be the original time, right? Has the house hold gotten out of Viet Nam?

I miss you very much!!! We are fine here in gramma and grandpa's house. All the people are worried about you, except me. I know if you have to you can get yourself out with other people or by yourself. I know you can take care of yourself. Make sure the mini-bike gets out. How are you doing with the radio problem? I hope you're o.k. and you do get the problem solved. I've got to go to bed now.

Good-bye and Good Luck

I love you very-very much,
Chris [age 14]

PART THREE

THE FINAL DAYS

A CLARIFYING NOTE

I was not on my father's evacuation and never heard a cohesive tale of events. However, I've read widely, visited the locations in Vietnam, and conducted numerous interviews. I have the collection of notes and letters he wrote during that time. Also helpful was the book written by his co-worker and station assistant Charles Eugene Taber, *Get Out Any Way You Can*.

With all these resources, I have—in what I hope is the best storytelling fashion—written a creative nonfiction narrative of the evacuation.

I took heart from Tim O'Brien's words, "that story-truth" can be as valuable as "happening-truth" and feel I have represented the spirit of the days on Phu Quoc in a genuine fashion.

On April 4, 1975, just as his ordeal was beginning, my father wrote that whether he made it or not, his attempt to get out of the country would be "an odyssey worth writing a book about." He never did write that book. I hope the one I've attempted does the job.

"A thing may happen and be a total lie; another thing may not happen and be truer than the truth . . .

I want you to feel what I felt. I want you to know why story-truth is truer sometimes than happening-truth."

– *Tim O'Brien*

From the chapter: How to Tell a True War Story

REGARDING IDENTITIES

Names that appear in quotes on the first reference are aliases. Many actual names appear in documents included in my writings but I've chosen to use aliases in this creative nonfiction version of the final days since some personalities are blended and some of the people were unavailable or unreachable for comment or collaboration. This story is based on truth but my representation of those involved is my own.

EARLY APRIL

The House Seven offices were always chilly, and James
Welch, U.S. Chief of the Mother Vietnam Propaganda
Radio Project, pulled his padded Middleton jacket
closer around him. A Christmas gift from his wife, its
blue and brown stripes reminded him of the happier
days on holiday in Thailand far from the pressures of
the Vietnam quagmire.

Now, he was seated across from "Roger Hellman"
and "Paul Edwards," two of his closest CIA compatriots.
His in-box nearly obscured Hellman's face, so Welch
leaned forward and put his elbows on the laminate top
of his government regulation desk.

James Welch (left)
and colleague receive
a Christmas gift from
his South Vietnamese
counterpart at House
Seven, 1972.

Hellman was the House Seven radio engineer and Edwards, fluent in Vietnamese, was the linguist, the gatekeeper for all Vietnamese communications coming in and out of the radio offices. Welch and Hellman were smoking Winstons down to their filters one after another, as if tobacco might solve the problem of a situation gone haywire. Edwards sipped laconically on a Coke.

Welch was just about to speak when "John Clemens," his deputy chief, walked into the room.

"Hello, John," Welch said. "Welcome back."

Hellman ducked his head in greeting while the more sanguine Edwards smiled broadly.

"We were just discussing the shithole we've found ourselves in. How was your family-leave time?" Edwards said.

Clemens pulled up a fourth chair and swept off his faded baseball cap. He was still on stateside time, his eyes bleary but bright. "It was great. Kids are great, but when I heard the latest news, I hightailed it back here. Didn't want to miss all the fun."

"Yes, fun," Edwards said. "The star of our show just told Jim that her father had a great plan for the end. He's going to pull out the rifle he's been hiding, shoot them all, then turn the gun on himself. Better than the alternative, he thinks."

"The alternative of being rounded up by the communists and being shot or else thrown into a 're-education' camp?" John replied with mock cheerfulness. "I'd have to agree. Anyone who's been working for us Americans can expect the worst, that's for sure."

Welch took another deep draw on his cigarette, then stubbed it out in the brass ashtray, pushing ashes over the edge and onto the well-worn desktop.

"The bigwigs are only providing for ten KIPs," Welch said, referring to the "Key Indigenous Personnel." House Seven had over 250 employees who fell into that category. Welch had long been a company man–well over two decades. And he had never once wavered in his patriotic duty to uphold the Constitution, protect his country, and to follow the commands of his ranking officers. But that was before he'd been thrust into the position of standing sentinel at the gates of a rapidly dis-integrating military situation that threatened the lives of the people he was also sworn to protect.

"Ten slots is nowhere near enough," he said finally. "We can't just ditch everyone here at the station. We can't just leave them to the commies."

"Did you see the news from Da Nang?" said John. "It's bedlam, people are literally dying—and killing—in their attempts to get out."

"Something to look forward to," Hellman said dourly.

"We've got to do better," said Welch, slapping the desk. "We just have to."

"I have an idea," Clemens said.

The three men looked at him expectantly.

"We have a transmitter down at Vung Tau. What if

we move the House Seven operations there under the guise of continuing our normal day-to-day operations?"

The room was silent as they each considered the popular beach resort less than two hours south of them. The wide modern highway would make for an easy drive from Saigon.

"That just might work," said Welch. "If we spin it just right, Polgar will be grateful for the opportunity to give our radio program a better-than-fighting chance of staying on the air. At least, better than it's going to be around here."

Tom Polgar was Siagon's CIA head honcho and a pretty surly type. Still, he liked the guys at House Seven, probably because Secretary of State Kissinger liked them, but clout was clout.

"Even if we get Polgar on our side, Martin will be suspicious," said Hellman, referring to the next higher-up, Ambassador Graham Martin. "He thinks Saigon is going to remain a bastion of democracy until the second coming. With all his high hopes of a negotiated settlement with Hanoi, we've got a snowball's chance of hell of getting permission from him."

"We'll just have to convince the both of them that this makes sense," said Welch, the wheels beginning to turn in his mind. "It just takes the right story, and that's what we're good at, isn't it?"

"Yeah, it's easy," said Edwards. "All we have to say is that moving the location of the broadcast operations will give us more power in maintaining our psywar efforts on behalf of the Thieu regime, not less."

The men laughed; it was a memo in the making.

Edwards went on. "Saigon is obviously being overrun with refugees from the North, and it's too hard for our people to get to work, to buy food, to maintain a normal lifestyle. Vung Tau will be much quieter and easier for our folks to focus on the important work at hand."

"Brilliant," said Welch. "But we've got to approach this systematically. We can't go right to Polgar and Martin. Let me talk to Richardson first. Is he around?"

"He's never around," said Hellman.

"Actually, I did see him downstairs," said Clemens. "I think he's here for his monthly check-in. Let's go take a look."

Welch and Clemens descended the narrow flight of stairs. "Gary Richardson" was there at the bottom, rifling through a stack of papers. "Hana Sang," the premier star of the Mother Vietnam radio program, stood beside him, patiently waiting.

"Gary, we need your help," Welch said without preamble. He paused, however, when Hana Sang said hello.

"Good morning, Jim," she said. "I hope you are doing okay after the departure of your family."

"Oh, hello, dear," he replied. "I am, I am. Doing okay. Thank you for coming to the airport this morning to see them off. Little Carla especially liked that."

Hana Sang smiled in reply.

"Look, I'm glad you're here," Welch said to her. "Clemens and Edwards have come up with a great plan for helping—" he hesitated, reminding himself that he was now running his own personal propaganda operation here. It wouldn't do to lay all the cards on the table. He gave Hana Sang a small shake of his head. A look flashed between them and she gave the slightest knowing nod. Richardson stopped shuffling the memos and looked up to meet Welch's gaze.

"Hello, James," he said. "Hello, John. What's going on?"

"Gary," said Welch. "We're looking to optimize our Mother Vietnam operations. We think that it might behoove us to look into other venues to broadcast from. As you know, Hana Sang here, and the rest of the crew, are struggling with the influx of refugees into the city. It's making it hard for them to get to and from work, and even to go shopping. We want to make it easier for them to concentrate on the important work at hand."

Richardson handed the sheaf of papers to Hana Sang. "Here, this is the memo I was referring to, right on the top."

He turned back to Welch. "You're looking out for their safety, aren't you?"

Welch hesitated, but only momentarily. "Yes," he replied simply.

Richardson was the CIA Base Chief and therefore oversaw multiple sites including the PSYOP radio program. He was often preoccupied with other duties, but he'd always had a soft spot for House Seven and especially Hana Sang and the other dedicated staff of the Mother Vietnam show.

"Well, you're damned right," Richardson snapped.

He turned an admiring gaze on Hana Sang. "We have to keep this little beauty out of commie hands."

Hana Sang beamed but dropped her eyes.

Richardson turned back to Welch. "What did you have in mind?"

"Moving operations south, to Vung Tau."

"Vung Tau?" said Richardson. "That place is as overrun with refugees as Saigon, or quite nearly. We need a better plan than that. Let me talk to some of our South Vietnamese officers and see if we can't find a better alternative."

◆ ◆ ◆

Two days later, Richardson barged into Welch's office without knocking.

"Jim," he said. "I've found a better location for your op."

Behind Richardson was "Colonel Tien " of the South Vietnamese Army. As Welch stood to shake hands, he folded the page in his typewriter so it couldn't be seen. It wouldn't do for anyone to know that he'd already begun preparations for the move. The letter to his wife listed just a few little things he gathered thus far like two tons of rice and 20 gallons of the aromatic Vietnamese fish sauce, *nuoc mam*.

Tien placed a map onto the corner of his desk. Simultaneously, Richardson and Tien pointed to a pale green island in a sea of white on the nautical map.

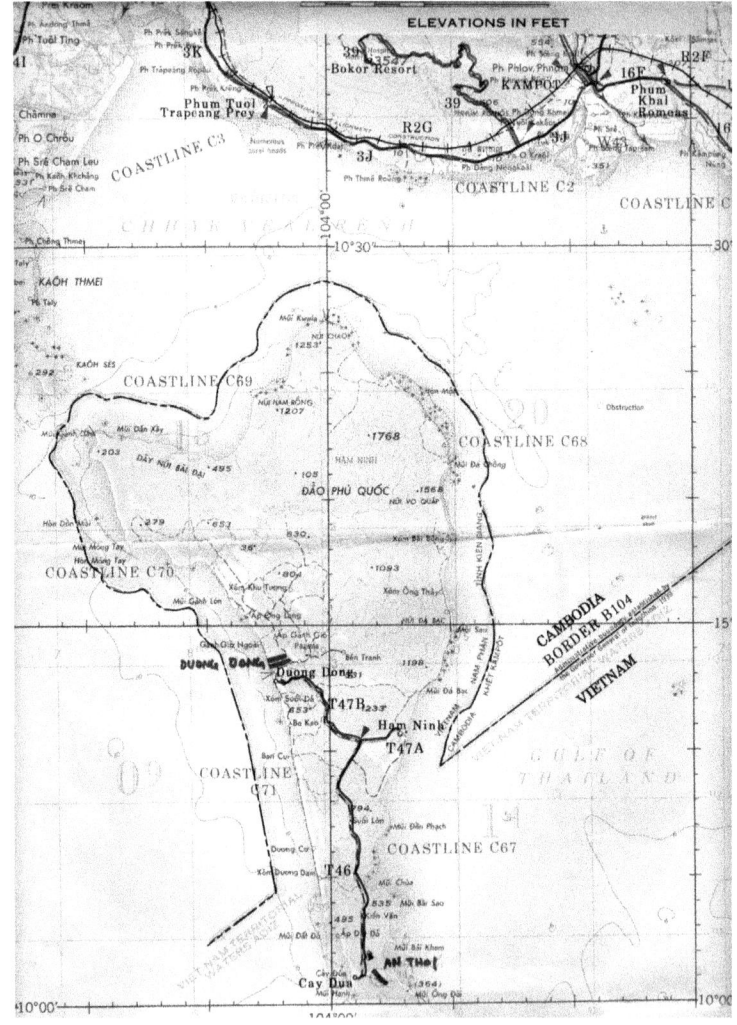

Phu Quoc," said Tien, clipping the second word so that it sounded like the syllable had gotten caught in the back of his throat. Welch again regretted that he'd never mastered Vietnamese as he had the German language in his early years.

"There are also many refugees there," said Tien in flawless English. "But it is not crowded like here or Vung Tau—"

"At least not yet," interjected Richardson with a quick shake of his head.

"There is an abandoned former US military camp," continued Tien, "that could work very well to make a place for the staff of House Seven to stay."

"And perhaps a few family members," Richardson added meaningfully. "A few."

Welch met his gaze and nodded. "We would be circumspect," he said. "Would the Station be able to provide any air support to get the staff, and, er, a few family members, down there? And, the equipment, of course."

"There is a Vietnamese naval base nearby," said Tien. "It has an airstrip that is in good working order."

"We can have some Air America C-47s

A 2015 Google Earth screenshot of Phu Quoc island assured me that the abandoned military base that housed "Camp Seven" was still there.

(left)

The map of Phu Quoc that South Vietnamese "Colonel Tien" gave to my father in April 1975.

available for use sometime in the next couple of weeks," said Richardson.

"That'll do," said Welch.

"The thing is," said Richardson, "it won't do for you to make all these plans without checking it out down there."

"I can go immediately."

"Let me get clearance from Polgar and Martin," said Richardson.

Both Tien and Welch looked at Richardson with raised eyebrows and pursed lips.

"Don't worry," added Richardson. "I know just what to say."

◆ ◆ ◆

Later that afternoon, Welch was rereading over his completed letter to his wife.

> *Your husband may be shot by the bureaucracy but I intend to get my people out regardless of the consequences. Talk now is of getting one million people out. I don't believe it. They may try and then cry and say we are sorry. I am not operating that way. I may fail, but I intend to do what is necessary before the crunch comes, and succeed. There are many details I can't write here for obvious reasons. If we make it, it will be an odyssey worth writing a book about–if we don't make it, it still will. All my love to everybody,"*

Richardson came in again without knocking.

"You've got the go-ahead."

Welch placed the letter face down on the typewriter.

"My God, you're a miracle worker. What did you say to convince them?"

"Well, it was just a matter of timing, really," said Richardson. "Both men are up to their eyeballs in crises, so I just timed my entrance to coincide with another officer's. They both trust me, and when I explained I was arranging for the safe and continued broadcasting of our critical propaganda efforts on behalf of the South Vietnam government, they gave me the thumbs up without another thought."

"Like I said, a miracle worker."

"Psychological warfare at its best," replied Richardson with a wry smile. With a sigh, he turned serious and pressed the door shut behind him.

"You know, Jim, this is going to be no laughing matter. Of course you do. I got you the permission you need so you're sanctioned to relocate now, but you're going to be on your own and under no circumstances are you to evacuate from Phu Quoc."

Richardson handed him a well-stamped memo. "Your orders from the Joint General Staff for travel to the island but with clear orders not to leave it. These should clear the way but I'd be sure that you and your men keep your handguns with you at all times. The infrastructure here is crumbling around our ears. Martin won't admit it, goddamn him, but we're in for a world of pain. You get your people out of here and God-speed to you. I'm going to stay here until I see the whites of their eyes but I'm not going to have the resources to help anyone else."

Welch nodded and Richardson shook himself like a dog shaking off an afternoon nap. "But first things first. I commissioned a turbo-prop to take you to Phu Quoc. Go any afternoon that suits you, you should be able to get there and back in a couple of hours."

Richardson moved to the door, then looked back at Welch who had picked up the letter to his wife and was rotating it end over end.

"Take especially good care of Hana Sang, will you? She's a national treasure."

Welch folded the letter in half and put it in his desk drawer. He nodded at his boss, "Don't you worry, Gary, I'll take good care of her. The best care."

APRIL 8

James Welch was up to his waist in boxes of trash bags
when the walls around him shook like the building was
coming down around him. His blood ran cold. Was he
too late? Had he waited too long? Was the North Vietnamese Army on top of them already?

There was a moment of eerie silence before another
overwhelming barrage of bombs caused the walls to
shake again. As he opened the door into the inside
hallway of House Seven's first floor, a sustained release
of heavy weapons fire roared from the streets outside.
His heart nearly stopped in his chest. It sounded as if
the city itself was falling. The building, old though it
was, was holding steady and Welch decided the sound
must be coming from all the machine guns sandbagged
in place at strategic intersections of the city.

Emerging from a studio just up the hall, Hana Sang
ran to him, her eyes wide and searching. He sponta-
neously embraced her.

"Thank God you're okay," he said over the noise.

She pulled back and gave him a quick, weak smile.

"That was a close one," she said. The gunfire was more
intermittent now. "We need to send a reporter to find
out what happened so that we may report on it in our
next broadcast."

"I'll get on the phone," Welch said. "I don't want anyone going out there until I know what's going on and if the danger is really past."

He took her hand and squeezed it. "Especially you, the star of our show."

Hana Sang smiled brightly and let her hand linger in his for just a moment. "We must all keep safe," she said. "You are a good boss to keep us safe."

Welch tried to smile back. It had been a tall order to begin with and it was getting taller by the minute.

It would be some hours before the House Seven staff would hear that the barrage had been caused by an attempted assassination of President Nguyen Van Thieu. A South Vietnamese regular had easily slipped a plane into the air and bombed the presidential palace and then just as easily taken the bomber safely to the North.

The ensuing gunfire in response had been nothing but an empty threat to the pilot, a guttural cry of frustration at the impotence felt by soldiers put in the impossible situation of protecting what could not be protected.

President Thieu had survived the attack by sheer luck, but Welch did not believe that luck would last. No one in their right mind did.

The Presidential Palace in 1970 which housed the residence and offices of President Nguyen Van Thieu.

APRIL 16

The stress of keeping the radio program on air while trying to plan the getaway took more time and energy than Welch had anticipated. He sure wished he had three or four other operatives to help with the preparations.

Still he kept at it, doggedly stocking up on basic supplies, packing equipment and furniture, holding regular trainings to go through the paces of evacuation, planning for every contingency. He directed Hana Sang and the singers and musicians to pre-record programs to air while they were in transition; he did not want Mother Vietnam to go silent at any time during the move. If the higher-ups got a single whiff of a crack in their plan, they could conceivably pull the plug on the whole operation. How long did he have? He just didn't know. Some thought Saigon would be safe well into the next calendar year, but he was not so hopeful despite his usual optimistic tendencies.

16 April

Dear Nance—

Where do I begin?? The last two weeks are so filled with action you would never believe it. I have just received your second and third letters and understand your concern. We are going along day by day doing what must be done and preparing for "tomorrow".

His fears were confirmed when he heard the news that the North's army was moving on Xuan Loc.

"That province is only 35 miles northwest of the city," said Hellman. "That's way too close for comfort."

"You got that right," replied Welch. "Order up a small plane. We need to go check out that island tomorrow."

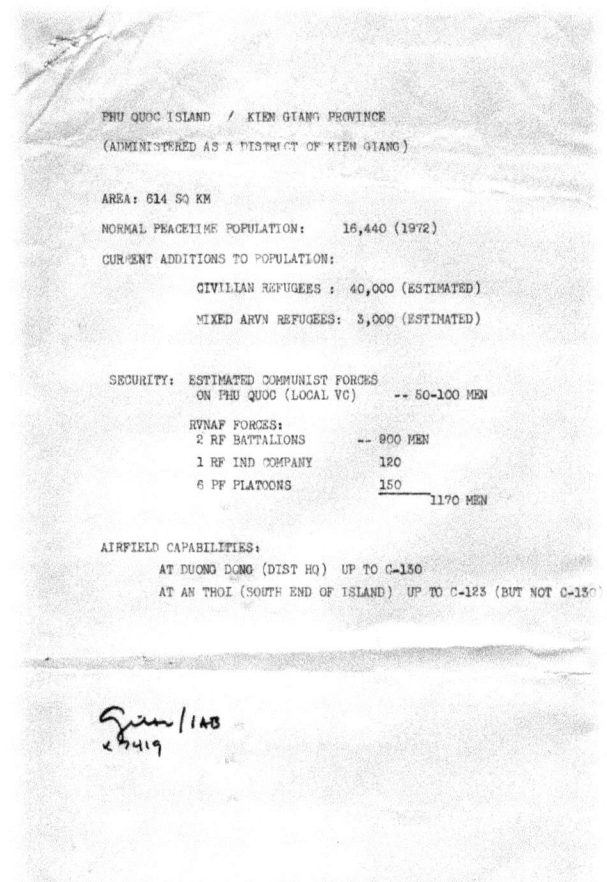

A situational analysis of Phu Quoc helped in the decision to choose it as a site suitable to "relocate the radio operations" of House Seven.

(left)
April 16, '75 letter home.

APRIL 17

Welch and Hellman stared soberly out the window of the turbo-prop plane, each lost in his own thoughts.

"Why all the long faces?" said their companion. They turned to him with questioning stares. "Jack Dobbs" just laughed. At 30-something, he was younger than them by far and had nothing to worry about but keeping all the radio equipment running smoothly. He cracked open a fifth of whiskey.

"Come on, guys, lighten up. We made it through the outgoing flak, didn't we? Thanks to our pilot's frisky flying." He took a swig and handed the bottle to Hellman. "Join me in a drink, won't you?"

Hellman looked to Welch who shook his head.

"You go ahead. I'll hold off but save some of it," he said. "Dinnertime's not all that far off."

◆ ◆ ◆

The landing was as smooth as the short flight and they were relieved to find someone waiting for them.

"Welcome to Phu Quoc, gentlemen," the uniformed officer said, extending a hand. "I'm 'Captain Thanh.'"

"Thank you for meeting us here, Captain. I'm James Welch, Radio Project Chief and this is Roger Hellman, my assistant, and Jack Dobbs, equipment engineer."

After shaking hands all around, Thanh led them to a waiting jeep.

"I am happy to show you around," he said. "Your telegram said that you were looking for someplace to set up a remote broadcast station?"

"Yes," Welch replied. "We feel that Saigon is getting too . . ."

". . . full of unwelcoming elements?" Thanh finished.

"Yes, you could put it that way," Welch said.

As they drove away, Thanh turned to look at them from behind dark glasses.

"The telegram also said you are looking for someplace to house . . ." he paused as if to double-check his memory. ". . . possibly as many as one thousand people?"

"Yes, that's right. One thousand," Welch replied.

"That is a lot of people to run a single radio show."

Welch chuckled. "Well, we don't know how long we'll be staying. Many staff members want to bring their families to make it more comfortable."

"Of course, I understand completely," said the captain.

He pulled off the highway and up to an elaborate gate with an empty guard room.

"One moment, gentlemen, while I unlock the gate."

Soon they were bumping down an overgrown and rutted dirt road, dodging potholes. The overgrown jungle gave way to a collection of cement buildings.

Thanh parked the vehicle and the four men got out.

"This is the abandoned military complex," he said. "I hope it will meet your needs."

It was a bit rough—doors hung sideways in their frames and window glass was shattered but there was a lot of space under the high roofs inside and the land immediately around the buildings was clear.

"This looks perfect," said Welch. "I think it could work quite nicely. There're places inside and out to serve as living quarters. Even plenty of wood from the forest for fires. What do you fellas think?"

Dobbs turned from scanning the tree line.

"It's not bad for a mess," he said. "It's not ideal but better than skinning a coon with a pen knife."

Thanh gave Welch a confused look but he just shook his head; ignore that reference.

"It will take a bit of spit and polish, but that will help keep everyone busy while we wait for what's to come."

"And what do you think that is?" said Hellman.

"I refuse to say," said Welch. "I'm just determined that we should all live through it."

"Come hell or high water," said Dobbs.

"Yeah, we got that, we got that much for sure," said Hellman.

As if to lighten the mood, Thanh walked to the edge of the forest.

"Come," he said. "Let me show you the beach."

After a few minutes walk, they emerge onto a beautiful golden sand beach.

"This is Khem Beach," said Thanh. "It is not as nice as Sao Beach to the north, but it could be used for bathing, and washing dishes and clothing."

"It's a damn sight more beautiful than Vung Tau," said Hellman. "If we'd known about this before, the entire front of the war would have shifted down here."

Thanh looked pleased and led them back to the jeep, their chatter markedly more upbeat than earlier in the day.

Another short ride and they had reached an elevated ridge just to the north of the compound. Here was another large concrete building, a prospect for a transmissions center.

"This is perfect," said Dobbs. "I love this goddamned place. I'll set up the transmitter right here, and we'll have the radio program spitting out our anti-commie message in no time."

"What about also using it as a communications center for contact with the embassy?" asked Welch.

"Piece of cake," said Dobbs. "Piece of cherry-pickin' cake. Let's get our crap down here ASAP; there's no use waiting when we got a set-up like this."

Welch could not help but feel ecstatic on the way back to Saigon. They would begin the relocation with all possible speed.

The following day, Welch met with Clemens, who agreed to travel ahead and set up the new digs. The House Seven staff would undoubtedly feel much more at ease knowing that a familiar face would be there to greet them. From overheard hallway conversations, Welch knew just how nervous many of them were. And no wonder, they were leaving their lifelong homes and extended families for who knew how long. Add to that, that some of them had never even left the city before, much less ridden on a plane and the whole operation became that much more monumental.

Chris with our black poodle Duffy on the roof of our Saigon house. He would be evacuated out via Pan Am on the day after my father left to Phu Quoc Island with his staff.

Clemens packed light, taking only two small bags and a favorite wooden tennis racket. If anyone at the Phu Quoc Naval Base were up for a game, he wanted to be prepared.

Accompanying Clemens to Phu Quoc was Dobbs with his entourage of radio-tech subordinates. They would begin the set up of the new radio broadcast headquarters so that, if all went well, programs could be aired from the new location even as the staff made their way down.

When Captain Thanh greeted them, Clemens could not help but notice that he was taller than the average Vietnamese man, and hoped that he had found his tennis partner.

APRIL 21

Monday, April 21, 1975, marked the beginning of an unusual work week. Even as South Vietnamese President Nguyen Van Thieu resigned and fled the country, many House Seven employees were taking courageous action and accepting Welch's invitation to fly south.

By the end of the day, nearly 300 staffers and their families had made their way to Phu Quoc. They had spent the prior days sorting through their many belongings, choosing what was so valuable that they would carry it into the unknown, leaving behind many treasured items they knew they would never see again. Since they were only allowed to bring a single bag each, many had sewn money into the seams of their bags and their clothing as a safeguard against uncertain times, a wish for a day when they would be able to begin their lives again. All of them had left someone behind—a parent, a grandparent, a sister, a son; the burden of seeking safety was a heavy one.

Hana Sang arrived at the airport accompanied by her father, a well-dressed man with a serious expression. He would not be going on the House Seven evacuation but he had business to attend to before he let his daughter proceed. He approached James Welch, who was studying a page full of cramped lines of writing.

"Good afternoon, sir," he said by way of getting Welch's attention.

Welch looked up and hurriedly extended a hand to "Mr. Khoy Nguyen." The two men had met before, of course, as Hana Sang's father was a director in the South Vietnamese government, but this meeting was unlike any other.

"Mr. Welch," said Nguyen. "I do not like that Hana Sang has chosen to stay with House Seven but I cannot

21 April

Dearest Nancy—

I am departing today for Phu Quoc Island with my whole staff. I have just paid off Hoa and gave her money for a plane ticket if she wants to join me.

Am taking Phuoc + Mai with me as well as Mai Lan so we may have new responsibilities when I get them evacuated.

Phu Quoc (southern tip) is about the most secure area in SVN now.

Must go love — saved your letters but have destroyed them so I have no answers now. More later. Love, Kim

prevent her decision. She has her own mind and I cannot change it. But I look to you, Mr. Welch, to take care of her."

Their hands were still clenched in a handshake. "I will protect her, Mr. Nguyen," said Welch. "With my very life should it come to that."

"We will stay in Saigon but leave as soon as the Ambassador allows us," said Nguyen. "I would like you to let me know immediately when you are in Phu Quoc and when you leave the island, if you do."

"We have orders not to leave the island," said Welch quickly. "We are to continue our broadcasts. But if we do, for some reason, I will let you know. You have my word."

Mr. Nguyen nodded gravely and led Hana Sang away for their own private good-bye.

Welch wiped his hand on his shirt. He was unsure if it was his sweat or Nguyen's, but he knew that he had made a promise he must keep, whether it cost him his life or not.

◆ ◆ ◆

The Nung Guards were a highly respected group of indigenous fighters. As such they were often employed by the U.S. armed services and the embassy. In this 1965 photo a Nung sentry is addressed by two Australian warrant officers.

On one flight, Welch dispatched a dozen Nung guards, courtesy of the Embassy. They were a minority ethnic group that lived primarily in the mountainous regions of Vietnam. Because their language was a dialect of Chinese—long-time enemies of all Vietnamese—and because they generally kept to themselves, they were considered an inferior race by most Vietnamese. U.S.

agencies had sought the Nungs out to serve as armed guards—they were good fighters, quiet, fierce, and loyal. These 12, with their M-16s prominently displayed, would monitor the entry points to the main camp and to the Comcenter, and be invaluable in ensuring the group's final escape from the island.

◆ ◆ ◆

Dobbs had made quite a bit of headway and had engineered the successful set-up of the Comcenter. Despite this, no communications were received from Saigon. Unbeknownst to the Phu Quoc contingent, all hell was breaking loose in the city. Xuan Loc, which had been under siege for nearly two weeks, finally fell to

the enemy, thereby removing all major blocks to a final advance on the South Vietnamese capital.

In addition, Thieu's resignation had been accompanied by a spate of accusations aimed at his supposed American supporters.

"The United States did not keep its promise to help us fight for freedom and it was in the same fight that the United States lost 50,000 of its young men," he said in a televised speech.

His departure cleared the way for the establishment of a leader that the communists might consent to negotiate with. By all accounts it was a little too late for that. However General Duong Van Minh or "Big" Minh, the ultimate appointee as the South Vietnamese leader, would do his best, but in a manner that would soon come as a surprise to all Americans.

◆ ◆ ◆

By the end of the relatively quiet day on Phu Quoc, portions of the stark gray buildings of the abandoned military compound had been modified into livable family-units using random pieces of cardboard, sheets, and blankets. There were small fires crackling between the buildings, with water on the boil for tea or rice. Some of the residents were perusing the provisions that had been delivered to the island with them. There was a generator but no fuel. There were pallets of food: bags of rice, crates of vegetables, and cartons of C-rations. Though not generally known for being delectable, the C-rations contained one treat that found favor. The children in the group were delighted to find cans of sweet fruit cocktail just waiting to be opened.

Someone had used the end of a burnt stick to make a sign: "Camp Seven." The place had been transformed and the roots of House Seven transplanted.

◆ ◆ ◆

Having no running water at first proved to be a challenge. The well at the camp didn't work and, though a naval truck provided potable water, it was a laborious process, keeping two people constantly busy filling and refilling barrels and tanks alongside the buildings. Because of this shortage, no one was to use the fresh water for anything but cooking and drinking.

Thus it was that the uprooted staff found themselves "stuck" with Khem Beach. While they washed and walked along the wide, long golden beach with its calm, turquoise waters, the world seemed as quiet and serene as the eye of a storm.

◆ ◆ ◆

Just before sunset, Welch, Hellman, and Hana Sang deplaned from a small executive aircraft to an empty air base.

"Well, this is a fine how-do-you-do," said Hellman, his single suitcase clutched in one hand and his briefcase in the other. The twin-engine aircraft was already taxiing down the runway to make its hour-and-a-half journey back to Saigon.

"It is very quiet," said Hana Sang, who also held just two bags, one bulging with clothes and personal belongings and the other full of notes and documents that would, perhaps, be useful in future Mother Vietnam broadcasts.

"Not to worry," said Welch, carrying a single bag of his own. "I'm sure everyone here had a long day. It's not a terribly long walk to the camp, we can use the exercise and fresh air after all these last weeks of being shut up in the office."

He reached out and took Hana Sang's suitcase.

"That is not necessary, Jim," she said.

"It will be easier for me to walk with one in each hand," he replied, his wry smile barely visible. "We'd best hurry before we lose all the light."

It was fully dark by the time the trio saw the lights of the fires in Camp Seven and, after a few moments of consternation when they were mistaken for intruders, they found their way to the living space at the end of the row of concrete structures that Welch had identified as the staff housing on his earlier trip.

"I will go find my Tran Li and set up camp with her," said Hana Sang. Tran Li was Hana Sang's close working companion and friend. Their voices sounded identical on air and the backup ensured there would never be a break in broadcasting.

Welch did not hand over her suitcase.

"No," he said mildly but firmly. "You are sleeping in the staff quarters with us. I told your father I would keep a close eye on you, and that is exactly what I intend to do."

In the dark of the night, with Saigon now so far away, and perhaps lost forever, the choice seemed absolutely clear, and the invitation-order a welcome safety net.

Hana Sang followed the two American men into the dilapidated concrete structure, where they all set up their makeshift beds of thin blankets and folded-clothing pillows on the hard floors and fell into the deep sleep afforded by exhaustion and each other's company.

APRIL 22

The next morning, Welch and Hellman made their way to the Comcenter on the ridge. Over steaming mugs of coffee, they briefed Clemens on the deteriorating situation in Saigon. After that grim analysis, they turned to a much more pleasing topic—that of the progress of their evacuation.

"Edwards is happy to handle the Saigon end," said Welch. "Since his family has already gotten away safely, he's set to stay in place and organize the remaining staff and their families into planeload groups, drive them to the airport, and see that they get aboard."

"One of our South Vietnamese staff members, 'Mr. Bui,' also elected to stay behind to help where he thinks it's most critical," Welch added. "It's a risky business, but he insisted."

No one said anything for a moment, each grappling with the gravity of the situation.

"I hope Bui gets out," Welch finally said, "but I do fear for him." He drained his cup of coffee. "Meanwhile, we've got work to do. When do the next round of flights begin, John?"

For the next two days, the skies would be abuzz with incoming Air America flights, transporting supplies, equipment, and people. Clemens continued as the point man at the airstrip, while Welch took over the management of the camp. With the size of the population growing by the hour, it was imperative to create an orderly structure to the days. Each of the ten buildings was assigned a number as well as a leader who carried the responsibility for communicating important messages to his residents, taking daily roll call, and enforcing an 8 p.m. in-camp curfew.

Welch held meetings with these leaders each morning to go over important items such as activities for the children, sanitation, cooking, and methods of communication. Hana Sang was a key player in helping the nervous Saigonese accept the strict and stressful rules of their new life. All of them had been accustomed to the freedom to live as they wished, but now, in the remote setting of the island compound, they were being treated almost like children—or prisoners. However, the uncertainty of their circumstances made them vulnerable in unprecedented ways.

The most pressing issue was security. Edwards sent regular handwritten reports each day by plane, which included intelligence updates.

"There is worry about our exposure to the 'elements' down there, especially the velocity count," he wrote. The not-so-subtle underscoring of the "v" and "c" was a reference to the threat of the Viet Cong. That Phu Quoc had been home to a handful of VC had been known, but they'd been believed to be sequestered in the remote northern end of the island. With the shifting political atmosphere, however, it seemed they might be making moves south. This, coupled with the very real threat that the local population and the South Vietnamese soldiers—all who would be left behind to face the communists alone—would soon become disgruntled, made Welch ever more happy that he had brought the Nung guards.

He instituted a strict camp entrance policy that involved the immediate appointment of a "movement control officer," whose first function would be to stamp an identification mark on the right palm of each person wishing to leave the camp.

"No person will be allowed to leave or enter the compound who does not have this stamp," he announced. "And since we are not yet familiar with the local milieu and geography, we must travel in groups of two or more. Contact with the local population should be minimized during marketing, and care should be taken that local people do not see the ID mark."

It was a system that seemed overly strict, even to him, but with Hana Sang's help in explaining the reasoning behind the enforcement of the policy, there was no protest. Indeed, with each passing day, the Camp Seven residents became more and more aware of their vulnerability.

When a CIA tape recorder went missing, Welch had to take an even stronger stance. He announced a policy that such crimes would be cause for immediate dismissal from the program.

"Such a transgression will ensure that the guilty person will not be admitted to the United States," he said. "In this first case, the culprit is invited to send the stolen item via a third party to myself and the matter will be dropped. We must insist on good order and discipline. Infractions will be punished by restriction to quarters for periods fitting the seriousness of the infraction."

This tension admittedly created a less-than-comfortable atmosphere, coupled as it was with the difficult conditions of sleeping on hard floors, having to boil all drinking water, limited food, few personal belongings, and only wood fires to cook by. Even Hana Sang's constant assurances could not assuage the tension that was beginning to infiltrate the camp. Upon her advice, Welch made it clear that anyone who was having second thoughts about the difficulty of the days ahead would be granted instant permission to return to Saigon.

◆ ◆ ◆

Meanwhile, in Saigon, the CIA staff who had been forced to stay behind were meeting challenges of their own. Officer "Harold Flynn" was nearly out of his mind with panic. He found his way to Ambassador Martin's office.

"Please, sir, we need to implement the evacuation strategy, Frequent Wind. It's time," he said, so upset that he barely stopped for a breath. "Haven't you seen the intelligence that's been coming in? Saigon is surrounded! An assault on the city is *imminent.*"

The ambassador smiled, took Flynn's arm, and led him back toward his door.

"Now, now, you're overreacting. It's natural for someone your age. Just keep your focus on your job and all will be well."

When the ambassador closed the door in his face, Flynn knew the conversation was over.

Flynn raced down the hall to Polgar's office but the Station Chief was just as unflappable as Martin had been.

"Here, look at this," he said, handing him a sheet of paper. "Everything is fine."

Flynn read quickly. It was a cable to Washington from the ambassador, sent just that morning. The intelligence evidence of any assault was simply a clever deception staged by the communists.

Flynn was nearly speechless. "What evidence do you have of a communications deception?"

Polgar waved his hand dismissively. "Please get back to work, Harold. You do have work to do, don't you? I am quite sure that both you and I will both still be in Saigon a year. At least I will be. If you don't attend to your work, I'm quite sure you may not be but not because of any farcical communist attack."

Flynn retreated, horrified. It was as if everything had gone crazy, simply crazy.

APRIL 23

On Wednesday, the first C-47 arrived with just 20 additional House Seven employees who were accompanied by a standard Army-issue jeep and a "buffalo"—a 1,000-gallon water tank.

The arrival of both vehicles had been eagerly anticipated, as they promised to make camp life markedly easier. Once they were deplaned by forklift, and the buffalo hooked up to a Navy truck, Welch, Hana Sang, Dobbs, and Hellman jumped aboard the jeep. It took a few tries, but Dobbs got the engine running and they headed to Camp Seven, feeling as if they were floating on air.

Once there, Welch unfolded the day's handwritten note from Paul Edwards. Hana Sang leaned in to read the note.

"What does it say?" she asked.

"Well, it looks like the embassy has eased its conscience by increasing immigration limits. They say they are going to allow 50,000 Vietnamese who've worked for us, plus relatives, into the States as immigrants."

"That is good," said Hana Sang, squeezing Welch's arm. "We are safe to be leaving then. They won't try to stop us."

Welch squeezed her hand back, but his focus was on the remainder of the letter. He let out a bark of laughter.

"Listen to this, Roger," he called. Hellman looked up from the jeep's engine. He'd been adjusting the carburetor settings, hoping to get it to run more smoothly. "Our House Seven evacuation plan is now being touted as a model by some at headquarters."

"Of course it is," replied Hellman sardonically.

"Oh, wait," added Welch, "Edwards says they might be thinking of using Phu Quoc as a possible conduit for shuttling more people out of Saigon. I don't know if *that's* good."

He read the rest of the letter aloud:

"It will burden our facilities and supply sources, but our recognition factor grows considerably, thus increasing the talk of getting a ship—of which there has been much. The more the merrier. So you see, Mama still lives in the hearts and minds of men."

"Mama?" said Hana Sang, quizzically.

"Mother Vietnam," replied Welch, kissing her lightly on the head. "You and Tran Li—the stars of our show. You made Mother Vietnam the show that remains alive even when some have lost all hope."

"Does this mean we don't need to find a ship all on our own?" broke in Hellman.

"Well, I don't think we should jump to conclusions," said Welch.

"Yeah, me, neither," said Hellman. "I already feel like a sitting duck."

Welch scanned the rest of the letter. "Edwards says the tension up there is almost palpable, 'Bien Hoa closed its doors and heavy shelling is expected any day.'"

"See, like I said, the good news never stops," said Hellman with a shake of his head. "So what shall we do?"

"Well, there's no definitive orders," said Welch, flipping the page to be sure there weren't any additional instructions on the back. "Edwards finishes with 'Saigon moves on as usual in the vacuum of political silence. But something is going to pop soon, just how soon is anyone's guess.' I sure wish he and Mr. Bui would get down here. I'm going to send a message back saying so."

"They'll stay to the bitter end," said Hellman. "You know how they are."

◆ ◆ ◆

The men and Hana Sang set about getting the water buffalo set up, as well as attending to the other daily tasks related to food, security, and community activities. As they worked, each one's head was spinning with questions: Were they going to receive additional airlifts of people? Should they wait for the Saigon Station to arrange a ship for them? The final shipment of equipment still hadn't arrived, but what was the point in transmitting now that it was almost certain that Saigon would fall—Bien Hoa had long been seen as the very last gateway to the city. Should they even bother holding up appearances? So well had they spun the yarn of continuing broadcasts that each of them had almost begun to believe that the story was true. As they worked away with Edwards's message echoing through their minds, it hit them fully for the first time that this was no round-trip.

By that afternoon, Welch had decided that it was necessary to share the news from Saigon. For some, it would mean additional family members would be free to relocate to the States. But with limited communication from Phu Quoc to Saigon, they would not know whether their extended family had heard of the additional spaces or if they were going to be able to take advantage of it. Also, some Camp Seven residents had begun to feel deeply homesick and very frightened about the uncertain journey ahead. It was only fair to give them all the information possible and to allow them to make the most well-informed decision possible.

At the community meeting, Welch stood on a wide wooden crate to gain the attention of the nervous crowd. The faces that looked up to him were both vulnerable and guarded, hopeful and cautious. He explained in English that they had received new information in the morning's plane, then made room on the makeshift stage so that Hana Sang could translate.

"Each family will have to make a decision in the very near future," he said. "Either to stay in Vietnam or to commit to the long, uncertain journey of seeking U.S. citizenship."

Hana Sang translated, and he continued:

"We came here to re-establish our operation," he said. "But since this planning was begun, political and military events have moved swiftly. The U.S. government has allowed for 50,000 Vietnamese who work, or who have worked, for the U.S. government to enter the U.S.

Each family must determine now whether it wants to enter the U.S. to live. If not, it will be provided transport back to Saigon."

After the announcement, there was a great deal of murmuring in the crowd, but many of the household leaders immediately hurried back to their dwelling places to talk over the news with their families.

Thirty-nine people brought their single pieces of luggage to the Camp's entrance for the shuttle to the airport. Welch and Hana Sang were there to bid them good-bye.

"Tell them we wish them well in their journey," said Welch, "and that we are not sure if they will be able to come back to Camp Seven if they change their minds."

Hana Sang turned to the small crowd. They were uneasy and edging toward the waiting truck even as she spoke.

"We are glad that you are following your hearts and strong convictions," she said. "We do not know how long we will be remaining here in Camp Seven. We will welcome you back, but you may not be able to return; there are so many uncertainties right now."

The somber group nodded and began to climb into the covered bed of the truck that would take them back to the airstrip.

"Be safe," she called, tears filling her eyes.

Welch put his arm around Hana Sang and steered her back toward the fires of the camps.

◆ ◆ ◆

Back in America, President Ford was doing his best to prepare the public for moving on, declaring the war in Vietnam as "finished."

"Today, America can regain a sense of pride that existed before Vietnam. But it cannot be achieved by refighting a war that is finished as far as America is concerned," he said in a speech at Tulane University.

In Saigon, the preparations for battle were ratcheting up as the 18 North Vietnamese divisions coiled themselves around the city like a snake preparing to strike.

"Camp Seven" required a great deal of management. My father's lists and agendas were long and detailed, ranging from "small" details such as sanitary napkins to major issues of addressing racial tensions.

APRIL 24

Just after noon on Thursday, April 24, Welch stood near the water buffalo, having a heated conversation with several of the House Seven staffers. When Welch saw his deputy chief approaching, he finished his conversation and gestured for Clemens to follow him into his makeshift quarters at the end of one of the nearby buildings.

Agenda

1. Nung guards are part of our community and must be treated equally. Your safety may depend on them. There have been frictions between N. guards and Vietnamese especially in matters of water distribution. We admonish all Vietnamese to create good relations with the Nungs - not opposition. It is for the good of all of us.

2. Since yesterday's meeting there have been two more grass fires. One endangered the latrines. There must be no more grass fires to get out of control.

3. Three safes must be moved into Bldg 5 this morning.

"The Vietnamese are mistreating the Nung guards," said Welch. "They're withholding rations and trying to block their access to the water."

"Not surprising," said Clemens. "They regard them as country bumpkins at best and an inferior race at worst."

"Well, it's not just a matter of general courtesy," said Welch. "Our lives may very well depend on the loyalty of these Nungs. If I were treated like that, I'd take off for the hills."

"Let's hope it doesn't come to that," said Clemens.

"Let's hope not," said Welch, scribbling a few sentences on a scrap of paper to use in his next meeting with the building leaders. "I'll make an announcement this evening."

Hellman and Dobbs appeared at the door to the building.

"What's the word?" said Dobbs. Without waiting for an answer, he continued, "We should be getting up to the Comcenter for our afternoon call with Saigon—if anyone's there to answer the other end of the horn, that is."

As they made their way to the jeep, Clemens recapped his news, adding that he was hoping the embassy had managed to assign a ship to their group.

"If they don't get us a ship soon, we're as good as stranded."

They connected to Saigon on the first try, and Clemens eagerly asked if they knew anything about transport for the House Seven group if things kept falling apart.

Saigon replied that they didn't know anything about a ship; in fact, the radio operator knew of no plans for helping the Phu Quoc contingent at all.

"Hang in," said the radio man over the crackling connection. "Just hang in."

"Well, that's sound advice," said Hellman.

The four exchanged weary looks and just shook their heads.

◆ ◆ ◆

Upon returning to Camp Seven, they found a written invitation awaiting them. Captain Thanh wondered if the Americans would like to join him and his family for dinner. They happily sent a reply in the affirmative, eager for a home-cooked meal and relaxing conversation on real furniture. Welch asked Hana Sang to join them, sure that the host would take to her as readily as everyone else did.

Captain Thanh greeted them at the door and introduced his wife, who was dressed in a traditional *ao dai* outfit. She spoke English and offered the guests a drink—would they like Cutty Sark or Budweiser? Clemens gratefully accepted a beer while the rest indulged in scotch with the Captain. Hana Sang followed her into the kitchen to chat and help out with the dinner preparations.

The men sank into comfortable couches in the living room with groans of satisfaction. It had only been a few days at camp, but they could feel it in every bone in their bodies. Captain Thanh raised his glass.

"Here's to your efforts on behalf of South Vietnam. I understand your radio broadcasts were very successful," he said.

"Yes, well, thank you," said Welch. "Our efforts did have some success, but obviously not enough."

"Unfortunately, the North has not complied with the ceasefire in the three years since it was signed. That has hardly been a recipe for lasting peace," Thanh replied.

There was an uncomfortable silence. There was still so much uncertainty about what was really in store for the country, no one wanted to delve into that can of worms during this welcome respite.

Thanh spoke again. "There is a Vietnamese saying, *Có chí làm quan, có gan làm giàu.* 'Fortune favors the brave.' I can see that you gentlemen value courage, for look, you have made your way down here away from the stresses of Saigon. May I ask that you allow me the same?"

The Americans looked at him questioningly.

"Should the time come when you head toward that horizon," Thanh said slowly, looking out over the bay. "May I ask that you take my wife and children?"

Welch exchanged a look with Hellman and Clemens. An unspoken message passed between them: we may already have too many people. However, they all knew that they needed to keep this man on their good side, for his help could prove invaluable in a crunch.

"Camp Seven" required a great deal of management. My father's lists and agendas were long and detailed, ranging from "small" details such as sanitary napkins to major issues of addressing racial tensions.

To-do list for April 24-25.

24, April ~~~~ 1000

1 Pay tomorrow out of petty
cash which will almost exhaust

2. Contractor bring written message
addressed Daddy - 2

3. Craft Departed 1300 w/2 pkgs
for D + 2

---

24 April 1630

1. Will ✻ respond in Writing to
Baker 1 - Charlie's Note received today
in writing.

2. Ship standing by - Charlie

---

25 April ~1000

1. PVN 50,000 advanced to Nung
Guards against salaries. PVN 16,000
to Nurses. Both groups should be
paid by Embassy soonest

"Of course, Captain. I could not refuse you that," said Welch. "But what of yourself?"

"I will not desert my post," Thanh said. "Many soldiers and officers have already, as you know, done exactly that but it is not something I can do in my heart."

"I admire that, Thanh. And yes, we will take your family, and one day you will be reunited with them when this war is behind us."

Thanh's shoulders dropped visibly with relief.

"I can't tell you, Mr. Welch, how much I appreciate that. And now that I know they are welcome with you and your group, I have news for you. Just today, an American ship has come into our waters. The U.S. American Challenger. Have you heard of it? It is a large ship and I will contact the captain for you. I am sure he will be willing to discuss a safe passage with you.

Welch, Hellman, Clemens, and Dobbs exchanged gleeful looks.

"That is good news, Thanh. Thank you!" said Welch, raising his glass. Everyone did the same and the glasses clinked merrily. Perhaps things were going to turn out okay after all.

APRIL 27

Life at Camp Seven became increasingly routine over the next several days. People were becoming accustomed to the rustic conditions and were finding their rhythm with collecting water, gathering rations, getting their hands stamped to take quick shopping trips to town, and washing dishes and bathing at the beach. The uncertainty of the situation became routine as well. Camp Seven residents brought their questions to the building leaders to be relayed to Mr. Welch, but Hana Sang, with her warm smile and reassuring voice, also became a go-to person. Welch did all he could to respond to each need and inquiry.

The question of when they would be getting off the island came up again and again, and the answer remained always the same. "It's unknown at this time. We are waiting on word from Saigon."

◆ ◆ ◆

On the evening of Sunday, April 27th, one of the sound engineers, Danh Zhen, approached Hana Sang and beseeched her to come and visit with him. He had made his own small encampment away from the family fires. She agreed without hesitation, as she had become a confidante to many and would not hesitate to help any of her comrades.

"I sit away from the others, so I can pray and meditate," he said as they lowered themselves to the ground near the light of his fire. He offered a shirt for Hana Sang to sit on, but she refused. Everyone had been allowed to bring so few belongings that it was not polite to accept the sacrifice of the use of their possessions.

"This is a very nice, quiet place," said Hana Sang.

"It has allowed me to see the truth, what it is that will help our group," Danh said. He looked from the fire into Hana Sang's eyes, his pupils dilated from the bright light.

"What is it? What do you mean?" Hana Sang said, leaning back slightly.

"I have had a vision that you must not sleep with the Americans tonight but you must sleep out in the open," he said. "The spirits that seek to protect us will come to you and tell you who in our group is Viet Cong. It is the only way that we can remain safe."

Hana Sang's breath caught in her throat. This was unprecedented and sounded dangerous. Still, she was very much committed to doing all she could to take care of the people that had come to Phu Quoc and who wanted so desperately to make it safely to a new life.

"I-I will think about it," she said finally.

Danh's eyes burned in the firelight, and he reached a hand toward her, grasping her forearm in a tight grip.

"It's the only way," he said. "I have seen many visions

but one never so strong as this. There are Viet Cong in our midst, and we must not let them surprise us and attack us in the night."

Hana Sang gently pried his fingers from her arm and stood. "I will think about this. I need to talk to my friend and we will decide."

"Do not delay," said Danh. "It must be tonight, or all is lost."

◆ ◆ ◆

Hana Sang hurried away and went to find Tran Li. When she explained the situation, Tran replied, "He is not a bad man, I do not think he is wishing to do harm with this plan. But it does not sound quite right. Do you think that you should perhaps speak with Mr. Welch?

Hana Sang nodded. "Come with me," she said. "I do not want to walk alone."

They found James Welch at the fire outside the American barracks, poring over a clipboard and smoking a cigarette with Hellman.

"Jim," she said. "I need your help."

He immediately threw his cigarette in the fire and reached a hand out to her.

"What is it, dear?" he said.

"I'm so scared. One of our sound engineers, Danh Zhen, just said that we must find out tonight who is the VC in our camp. He said the only way is for me to sleep outside and not in the building here with you and

Mr. Hellman. He said if I sleep out under the stars, I will receive a vision and then I can save the camp from betrayal by the Viet Cong."

Welch's face went white.

"No, Hana Sang, no, that is absurd."

"But, Jim, I must help if I can. I cannot allow any House Seven person to be hurt.

Welch reached into his briefcase and pulled out his handgun. He held it toward her, butt first.

"Hana Sang, if you want to do that, you'll have to shoot me."

It was Hana Sang's turn to blanch. "What, Jim, why?"

"Because I told your father that I would take care of you, and if you go and sleep outside unprotected, then you had better just kill me first because if something happened to you, your father would never forgive me."

Hana Sang stepped back, refusing to take the gun. She looked at Tran, who gazed back at her, giving a nearly imperceptible nod.

"Okay, Jim, I will tell Danh that it is not possible. I would not be able to hurt you, our leader, in order to find out who is a danger to our group."

Welch put his pistol away and reached out to the nearly weeping deejay. He hugged her tightly. "You are not responsible for finding the VC. That is our job. Your only job is to keep doing what you are doing by being a friend to everyone. Danh is out of his mind to ask such a thing. There are no visions to be had, only common sense to follow, and it is common sense that you stay safe indoors and by my side."

Hana Sang nodded and pulled away, suddenly embarrassed that she had lost her composure and good sense.

"You are right, of course," she said. "Tran and I will go to tell him that it is not possible."

"Be sure to tell him and hurry right back," said Welch. "Curfew is almost here."

APRIL 28

Late in the morning on the 28th, Captain Thanh stopped by Camp Seven to let the Americans know that the ship had arrived, and for better or for worse, it was in the process of unloading several thousand refugees from Vung Tau in landing craft that he had provided.

The ship was the American Challenger, a 21,000-ton U.S. Lines freighter under contract to the U.S. military for Vietnam evacuations operations. Welch and Clemens consulted and decided that Clemens could handle making contact with the ship's captain, while Welch continued to correspond with Edwards in Saigon.

Clemens took a launch out to the ship and met up with Captain Arthur Boucher. Over a steaming cup of bitter galley coffee, they discussed the situation.

"Were you sent specifically to take us off of Phu Quoc?" Clemens asked.

"No," replied Boucher, "but if I get the okay from Saigon, I'll be happy to."

Clemens considered. "We haven't had the greatest luck getting through to the command center in Saigon. The situation seems pretty chaotic up there, to put it mildly."

"I understand," said Boucher, "but I'd like to keep

our routines as close to standard protocol for as long as possible."

"I'll get back to shore and begin right away," said Clemens. "Can we reach you by radio all day?"

"I'll keep my radio man on standby, awaiting your call," said the captain.

They shook hands, and Clemens stepped onto the launch with a barely suppressed smile. How could the embassy *not* give permission? It only made sense that they would want the House Seven contingent to use the available ship. It was such a relief to know that they had a way off the island, avoiding the influx of the additional refugees slated to be housed in the compound just north of Camp Seven. If things got as crazy as they had in Da Nang, they could be sure that that group would overrun their now well-oiled living conditions. Clemens breathed the sea air deeply into his lungs. Things would work out, they just had to.

◆ ◆ ◆

Not long before sunset, a random load of 17 Vietnamese staffers from Rach Gia, a U.S. base on the Mekong Delta, landed at the Phu Quoc airstrip in a Chinook, a twin-engined, tandem rotor, heavy-lift helicopter. Paul Edwards' prognosis had been correct—the Embassy was beginning to use Camp Seven's base as a staging area for further evacuations. It seemed that the Ambassador had finally decided to begin getting people out of harm's way.

Unfortunately, his decision was too little, too late, for, just before sunset, five North Vietnamese jet trainers cum light bombers—Cessna A-37 Dragonfly fighters—circled above the Tan Son Nhut airport near Saigon and pelted the runway with bombs. One was piloted by Nguyen Tran Trung, the dissident who had bombed the Presidential Palace 20 days before.

But that was just the beginning. Those in Saigon endured a horrific, teeth-rattling assault on the airport. It was bombarded throughout the night and much of the following day. The runways were completely destroyed. There would be no more fixed-wing airlifts out of the city. Helicopters had become the only way out. But not for long.

APRIL 29 — EARLY MORNING

It wasn't until the morning of Tuesday, April 29, that Camp Seven heard that the true end was in sight. Unbeknownst to them, an order had been issued the day before for all Americans to leave the country within 24 hours."

It wasn't a notice from headquarters but a report on Radio Saigon, a general news broadcast, which replayed the speech given the day before by General "Big Minh." He had accepted the role of interim South Vietnamese President and was ready to negotiate the end of the hostilities with North Vietnam. To that end, he sent the following message to Ambassador Martin.

> Dear Mr. Ambassador:
>
> I respectfully request that you give an order for the personnel of the Defense Attache's Office to leave Viet Nam within twenty-four hours beginning on April 29, 1975, in order that the question of peace in Viet Nam can be settled early.

They were all stunned. Why hadn't they heard this directly from the Embassy? It was hard not to feel completely abandoned.

Welch called an emergency meeting with the Camp Seven community leaders and, with Hana Sang's help, dampened down the inclinations toward panic. No one had been happy to hear that there was no going back now.

"We should head up to the Comcenter," Welch said to Hana Sang when the briefing was complete.

As they turned to leave, one of the Mother Vietnam reporters stepped up.

"Excuse me, Mr. Welch," he said.

Welch turned to see *Xuan Le*, an even-keeled fellow who'd been a quiet and diligent worker over the years.

"May I join you?" he said. "I would like to see this for myself. As a reporter, this feels like an important moment to witness. I will not be a problem."

"Of course, Phien," said Welch. "You're absolutely right about that. This moment is going to down in history."

The three of them jumped into the jeep and headed up the hill. When they entered the center, Clemens was on the radio trying to make contact and Hellman and Dobbs were standing by, hands on hips.

"Diamond Control. Diamond Control. Come in. Over," Clemens said urgently, sweat running down his face.

Dobbs looked at Welch. "He's been at this for a while now."

For a moment, there's only static. A word or two breaks through.

"Diamond Control here. Please identify yourself. Over."

The men nearly let out a cheer but contain themselves; there's no telling how long the connection might last. Welch feels both Hana Sang and Phien grab his arms and he responds by gripping both of theirs in turn.

Clemens replied, his voice barely in control. "Diamond Control, this is House Seven South on Phu Quoc Island. Over."

"Roger that, House Seven South. Sorry about the com troubles. A goddamned tree fell on our antennae early this morning. We're holding things together with spit and bubble gum. Over."

"Roger that, Diamond Control," said Clemens. "We are requesting permission to use the American Challenger to evacuate our staff. Over."

There was a long pause and no one took a breath. Finally, the radio squealed and the radio operator responded.

"We cannot advise. I repeat, we cannot advise. Things up here have fallen apart a little sooner than expected. Tan Son Nhut was destroyed by the enemy early this morning and the temperature up here is 105 and rising."

"Are you serious, Diamond Control?"

"That's an affirmative. The ambassador has initiated evacuation protocol. The situation is entirely in the hands of the military now. We have no advisement for you."

Static ensued once again and the voice at Diamond

Control faded until it could barely be heard. "That's it, over and out."

Just before it went completely dead, a final faint message reached them. "... and good luck."

The room was dead still.

Welch sucked in a breath. At least they knew where they stood now. He realized he was clutching Hana Sang and Xuan Le's arms much too tightly and he broke the grip but took their hands. They all needed strength

To-do list prior to leaving Saigon for Phu Quoc. Note that no. 9 indicates he must take the Joint General Staff's orders that he and his staff were not to leave Phu Quoc Island.

(right)

Receiving this letter from a writer on my father's staff in 2005 sparked a reawakening and a confirmation: all those varied and randomly told stories of our childhood were true.

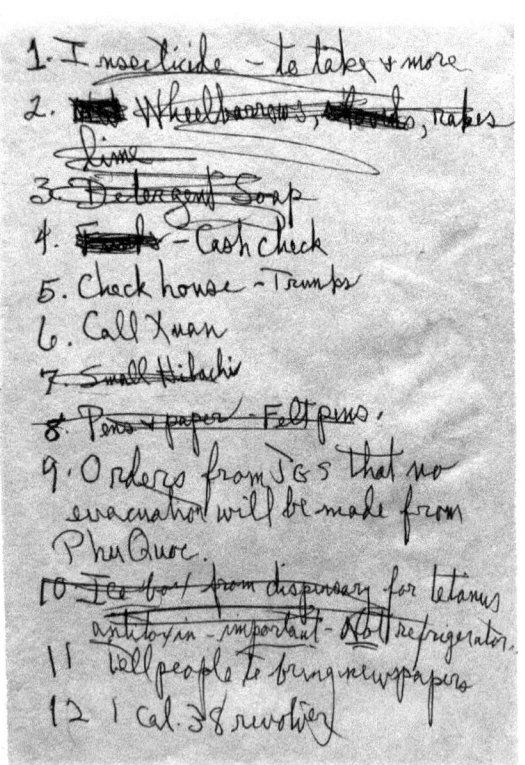

from each other. He looked at Dobbs and Clemens and Hellman.

"Well, you heard the operator. Let's go."

As he looked at each one of them, his eyes came to rest on Xuan Le's. Here was the very type of person he had done all this for. Hana Sang could have gotten out with her father. All of his American co-workers could have left alone on earlier transports. Xuan was a young man with his whole life ahead of him, a life that deserved a world without communist rule. Welch squeezed his hand as they moved toward the door.

"Let's go, Xuan" he said. He motioned with his head, indicating everyone to follow.

"Let's go. And I do hope luck is with us!"

One thing I wouldn't never forget your father was the moment of pandemonium of the fall of Saigon, in the radio room at Phu Quốc island, we received the ultime message from the US Embassy : « Go and Good luck » your father hold my hand and said : « Well let's go Phien ! » then he quietly smiled and added : « I hope luck is with us ! »

APRIL 29 — MID-DAY

As Saigon was signing off, it became clear to everyone on Phu Quoc that now was the time to make moves. Notification was received from the U.S. American Challenger had consented to load the House Seven group on the ship without waiting for permission from Saigon. Due to the shallowness of Cai Dira Bay, the ship would not be able to approach and dock near land. Therefore, in addition to the need for land transportation, it would be necessary to get water transport to the ship from the beach, but that was no longer an easy task.

The news of the Americans' ejection had the entire population on edge. It was clear now that within hours, the Northern communists would take control of Saigon

1. WITH RECEIPT PRESIDENTIAL MESSAGE ADVISING THAT EVACUATION AMERICAN EMBASSY SAIGON MUST BE COMPLETED BEFORE 0345 LOCAL TIME 30 APRIL, WISH TO ADVISE THAT THIS WILL BE FINAL MESSAGE FROM SAIGON STATION.

2. IT WILL TAKE US ABOUT TWENTY MINUTES TO DESTROY EQUIPMENT. ACCORDINGLY BY APPROXIMATELY 0320 HOURS LOCAL WE MUST TERMINATE CLASSIFIED TRANSMISSION.

3. IT HAS BEEN A LONG FIGHT AND WE HAVE LOST. THIS EXPERIENCE UNIQUE IN THE HISTORY OF THE UNITED STATES DOES NOT SIGNAL NECESSARILY THE DEMISE OF THE UNITED STATES AS A WORLD POWER. THE SEVERITY OF THE DEFEAT AND THE CIRCUMSTANCES OF IT HOWEVER WOULD SEEM TO CALL FOR A REASSESSMENT OF THE POLICIES OF NIGGARDLY HALF MEASURES WHICH HAVE CHARACTERIZED MUCH OF OUR PARTICIPATION HERE DESPITE THE COMMITMENT OF MANPOWER AND RESOURCES WHICH WERE CERTAINLY GENEROUS. THOSE WHO FAIL TO LEARN FROM HISTORY ARE FORCED TO REPEAT IT. LET US HOPE THAT WE WILL NOT HAVE ANOTHER VIETNAM EXPERIENCE AND THAT WE HAVE LEARNED OUR LESSON.

4. SAIGON SIGNING OFF.

and therefore the entire South. Those on Phu Quoc were either residents who would resent the Saigonese contingent boarding a ship to relative safety or refugees from Vung Tau, who would also resent what they would perceive as a privileged getaway by other Vietnamese. Additionally, the Viet Cong on the north end of the island were certainly getting ready to mobilize—if they hadn't done so already.

Welch consulted with the others and they agreed that all movement should take place after dark, when the island residents would be under curfew. Thanh had offered the use of only five trucks, which they estimated would be able to transport the nearly 1,000 people of House Seven in three groupings. It would be a tight fit, squeezing almost 70 people on each truck. All baggage would have to be transported separately; each person would only be allowed to carry a small bag or item with them so that they could all fit. However, the threat of being stuck on Phu Quoc would give everyone the motivation to squeeze together.

By the end of the day they had also received permission to use three landing craft utility boats—one standard LCU and two smaller LCM 8s or "Mike Boats," which were generally used by the military to transport equipment and troops from ship to shore. Each boat would make one trip to the freighter waiting offshore and would offer no seating or amenities, but they were seaworthy and would keep the group afloat.

My father carried this copy of CIA Station Chief Tom Polgar's last message out of Saigon through the evacuation and beyond.

◆ ◆ ◆

Evac Plan

1. Landing ship from Vung Tau arrives - Mon. PM. - Tues PM

2. Evac Freighter arrives Mon PM - Tues AM.

3. Cargo is transferred from Landing Ship to Freighter - Tues.

? 4. Welsh + Thien visit carrier + plan evac with Capt. of Vessel. Brief principals - Tues.

5. Load + transfer equipment + pers. effects via VN Navy lighters. Tues. Place aboard ship.

6. Wed AM - Both ships put out of Cay Dua and put into Bai Theo ?Kham.
   PM 3:00

7. Wed AM - House by house people will go to beach "for a swim". Landing ship puts into shore and all personnel board. Transfer is made to Evac ship standing off shore.

A detailed list of the orderly evacuation plan my father was hoping for.

It wouldn't be until much later that they would get word of what happened to Paul Edwards and Mr. Bui on this day. The two were supposed to have flown down to Phu Quoc on April 28 but had stayed to help with the final destruction of documents, not knowing that the airport would soon be bombed into smithereens.

On the afternoon of the 29th, Edwards was ordered to board a helicopter leaving from the roof of the Duc hotel. Due to the limited seats available, however, a decision had been made restricting the transport of any Vietnamese personnel out of Saigon: only Americans were to be airlifted.

As he was heading toward his rooftop transport, Edwards had no choice but to turn to Mr. Bui, shake his hand, and wish him the best of luck.

"I wish you were an American, Bui," said Edwards. "I am sorry that you and I must part here."

For both, it was an unbelievable moment. For Edwards, it was devastating. For Bui, it was devastation—he was being left behind. After all his dedication, he was being left behind!

"I did not desert, but I was deserted," he wrote in a story describing his abandonment and ordeal. "I felt sour and bitter in my heart. Had I not been in association with the Americans for 20 years, had I not worked for the U.S. Government for the most part of my life, I and my family would have comfortably stayed in our country with the communists like millions of our compatriots could . . ."

APRIL 29 — 8 P.M.

After curfew, Dobbs was elected to escort the trucks
from the naval base through An Thoi, making sure
along the way that the roads were clear. It was slow
going, the convoy making its way cautiously through
the deserted streets with the headlights off. Dobbs
found the roads were unobstructed and the town was
ominously quiet. The curtains were drawn in each
home, but he saw the occasional slit of light emit as
one drape or another was pulled aside as the rumbling
trucks passed by. The townspeople were obviously on
edge, wondering if this break in curfew signaled immediate danger, or was there yet more time before their
world came crashing down around their ears.

It felt very late by the time all the trucks pulled up
before the dark buildings. The group was surprisingly
reluctant to go, fleeing for their lives though they were.
The camp had become a familiar sanctuary in the wake
of leaving Saigon; they had started out with almost
nothing but had created a fairly comfortable set-up by
the end. Now, leaving their cold cooking fires and makeshift dwellings, they were keenly aware that they were
entering into the unknown yet again—this time with
even more uncertainty about the chances for success.

Despite their fears, they pressed *en masse* to scramble

Due to the location
of the "getaway
boats," my father
and his staff had to
drive through the
southernmost town
of An Thoi. He
had hoped to avoid
the risk of alerting
the locals to their
evacuation.

198

aboard. Each person clutched what they could in their hands—they had been instructed only to bring one small carry bag or item. They could only glance long-ingly at the rest of their worldly possessions stacked in a pile between the buildings. They were promised that Dobbs would follow with them later.

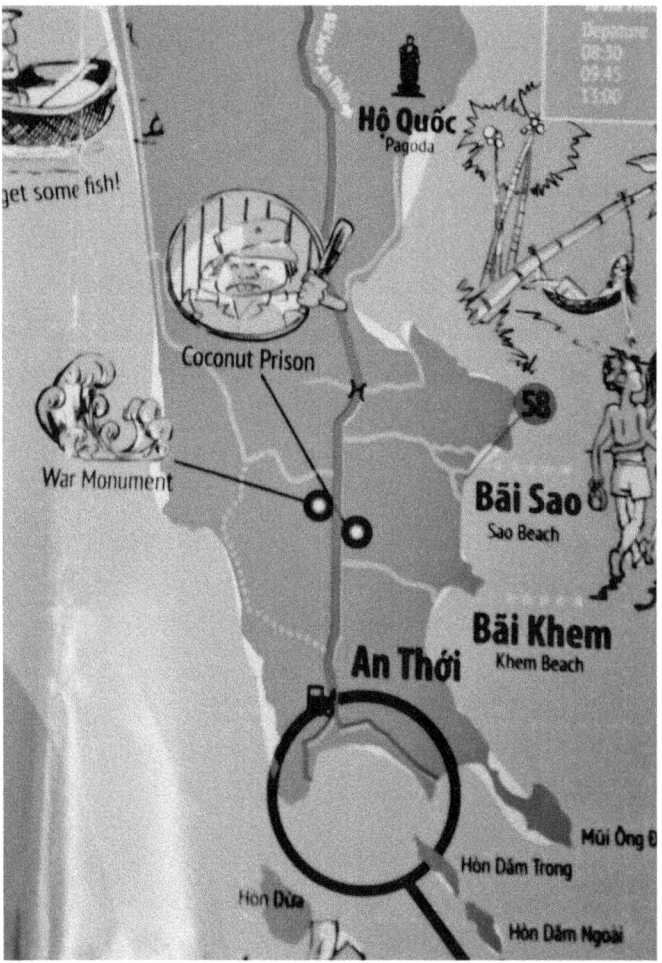

Welch and Clemens decided to split the group between them, with Clemens' contingent of about 600 heading out first in two truck relays. They would take a single boat, the larger LCU. Mr. Giang would accompany him as translator and return with the trucks to join Welch for his trip. At Welch's behest, Dobbs stationed some of his technicians at the Comcenter and more guards at the lower camp so that any locals who noticed would think that there was still an additional group to transport. This might help delay any negative response that might be brewing.

Clemens' Navy driver guided them easily to the beach just west of the airstrip, where a large landing craft was waiting with its bow door open and a landing ramp down.

"My group of six hundred will be able to fit," thought Clemens to himself, "in a pinch."

Two spotlights on the bow of the utility boat illuminated the beach area in front of the landing ramp where several Vietnamese sailors stood smoking. Groups of army soldiers stood clustered off to either side of the boats, doing the same. No one greeted Clemens as he walked down the beach alone toward the landing craft.

There was no sign of Captain Thanh or Commander Dao, and no one seemed to be in charge. Feeling uncertain but determined to move forward, Clemens returned to the trucks and instructed those aboard to unload so that the convoy could return to the camp for another load of passengers. They did so, then huddled nervously at the top of the beach, just 50 yards from their last transport to freedom.

Clemens decided that his only choice was boldness, and he began to lead the group toward the waiting boat. Within seconds, the troops on the beach closed ranks and spread out in a line in front of the LSU ramp, their M-16s poised for action. An officer appeared suddenly in front of the line of soldiers.

Clemens motioned for Giang to join him. He walked up to the officer and explained that Captain Thanh had authorized this transport for them. The officer said he had no notice of any such thing. He said he could not allow Clemens and the group to board.

Clemens felt a cold thread of fear filter through his veins—this had been his greatest fear, to be caught in the open with no defenses, and with the long-sought prize so close at hand. Worst-case scenarios began to flash through his mind. This group of soldiers may have gone rogue, opting for an every-man-for-himself survival tactic. Or it could be a Viet Cong trap. Or perhaps even an organized ARVN effort to collect bargaining chips— some Americans and hundreds of Vietnamese collaborators. What favor would that not win them when the regime change came?

Clemens took a deep breath and swallowed his fear. "Please, take me to see your commanding officer, I am sure he will understand."

The officer considered for a moment then nodded slightly and led Clemens and Giang to a jeep just beyond the Camp Seven huddle. Clemens heard the jittery whispers of worry as he passed by.

"Don't worry," he said. "Everything is going to be fine. I'm going to secure our permission to proceed. Please, everyone, take a seat on the sand. I will be right back."

In a matter of minutes, the trio pulled up to a one-story wooden building that was lit only by kerosene lanterns and furnished with simple tables serving as desks. The major on duty denied any knowledge of the orders allowing the Americans to use the LSU.

"I must phone Captain Thanh," he said in accented English.

The major cranked the field telephone on his table-desk. It took three tries before he reached the Captain's office. "He is not there," he said after a short conversation.

Clemens felt a line of sweat trickle down his spine. "Try Commander Dao," he beseeched. The major got Dao on the line after one good crank and proceeded to chat for what seemed to Clemens to be an inordinately long time. Finally, the major hung up.

"It is okay," he said with a smile. He turned to the officer from the beach and delivered his orders in Viet-namese. After saluting, he gestured for the two House Seven staffers to follow him back to the jeep. Before turning to go, Clemens extended a hand to the major.

"It is okay," the major repeated as he shook Clemens's hand. "It is okay."

By the time he returned to the beach, the second

round of evacuees had arrived. They'd obviously learned of the story of the delay for, with Clemens' return, the anxious faces of the entire group turned toward him. When he nodded, their expressions turned to joy, and once the officer ordered his soldiers aside, the group quickly crammed aboard the LSU. Clemens was the last to board, just finding enough room to squeeze into a gunwale to one side of the bow door. He waved good-bye to Mr. Giang as they pulled away from the beach onto the calm sea.

He felt like he had just enough time to begin to breathe again and to admire the stars above when he noticed a staffer pushing his way through the packed mass. What could it be now? The staffer said that he was wanted on the bridge immediately, and so Clemens climbed out of his perch and pushed his way through the crowd. As he was making his way, he noticed that the other boats in the harbor were going dark. When he got to the bridge, the captain pointed to the starboard side. A small boat was traveling parallel to the LSU.

"It is Captain Thanh," he said. "There are rumors that he is running away. Panic is coming." He waved to the disappearing lights. "They are putting out their lights to be prepared."

He pushed a bullhorn into Clemen's hand. "You must speak to him. It is not my duty."

"Hello, Captain Thanh," Clemens called.

"Mr. C, is it going well?" came Captain Thanh's voice over the water.

Clemens assured him it was, and Thanh then asked if it was okay for his wife and two children to board.

"Yes, of course," replied Clemens. "Just them?"

"Just them," replied Thanh. "Just them. I will return to shore."

The LSU slowed so that the boats could safely come alongside each other. Clemens greeted Thanh's wife and children as they scrambled quickly aboard—their goodbyes must have been made long since. Thanh called a loud thank you and quickly turned his boat away with only a short salute of farewell. Clemens waved good-bye to the receding figure, knowing that it was likely that he would probably never see or hear from him again.

APRIL 29 — 10 P.M.

Once Clemens was underway, Giang climbed back aboard the truck and he and Dobbs headed back to camp to load the second group. Welch was waiting there for them, and they quickly loaded the remaining evacuees.. There were only about 350 in this crew, including Welch, Hellman, and Hana Sang. His trusty Nung guards were the last to board, their M-16s slung over their shoulders.

As soon as they arrived at the beach, Welch noticed the lack of lights on the water. Something was going on—ships at sea did not put their lights out unless they were expecting an attack. Before he could make up his mind about what was going on, Giang informed him that the group was unloaded and ready to go. He had told Welch of all that had happened with Clemens, but they felt certain that Clemens' efforts had sorted things out for good, and they immediately began loading the two waiting Mike boats. Just as Welch was about to breathe a sigh of relief that they had made it so seamlessly, an armed naval guard approached from the checkpoint and called out rapid-fire orders in Vietnamese. Sergeant Giang stepped forward to translate. Apparently, no orders had been received allowing for *these* boats to depart.

"Tell them we have permission," said Welch to Giang. "Captain Thanh okayed the trip this morning. My God, Clemens' boat just left. Why can't we just follow?"

The guard and Giang exchanged several heated sentences. The guard motioned to a subordinate who took off in double time toward the gate at the top edge of the beach. He returned moments later. No one could find Thanh; rumors had it that he had left the jetty in a motorboat with his family sometime after Clemens had departed.

When Giang translated this, Welch's heart dropped. Without the usual rules of order in place, a situation like this could spiral out of control very quickly and his group could be slaughtered where they stood—spread across the decks of the landing crafts—so close to escape and yet worlds away. Just as he was contemplating this, a military truck pulled up and a dozen South Vietnamese soldiers poured out and ran up to the lead guard, who barked out a command. They quickly filed into place in front of the two landing boats. Welch eyed the M-16s clutched in the hands of the uniformed men. He had never seen guns look so menacing.

The Nung guards had not boarded, and Welch could feel their presence pressing forward behind him. He held up a hand to stop them. "Tell them we understand, Mr. Giang," he said. "Tell them we will get off the boats and wait for the orders to come. Please ask him to radio Commander Dao, he should have the orders we need."

After dispatching the guard back to the kiosk to

radio the commander's office, the soldier turned to the boats and yelled an order down the line. Giang quickly repeated the message in Vietnamese, but no one needed a translation. The guards were already stepping onto the boat ramps and motioning people to get off the landing crafts, using the muzzles of their guns as prods.

The group silently scuttled off the LSM-8s, their half-exhaled sighs of relief now bitterly caught in their throats. Was this going to be the end for them? Welch did his best to portray calm, even as he reached for his .38 pistol. Such a little handgun would not stand up against the power of an M-16, but should a shoot-out ensue, he could take out the spotlights, perhaps saving the lives of a few of his people before his own was ended. He motioned for Hellman and Giang to follow suit, pointing at the lights to indicate his meaning. They both nodded in understanding.

The Nungs pressed forward again, and this time Welch indicated that they take up positions between the South Vietnamese soldiers and his own people. As his guards stepped into position, their faces blank masks, the huddled mass drew closer together, making way for them, glancing at them with grateful looks. There was no maligning the minority men now.

Every uniformed man on the beach, naval and Nung alike, held their M-16s at the ready, and Welch felt the sweat pouring down his back. Where were the orders? It was a simple thing, one radio call should do it, but he knew when systems began to crumble, nothing could be counted on. With the end so near, the chain of command was disintegrating. The Vietnamese soldiers were just as afraid for their lives as he was, as his people were.

He crouched next to Hellman, Hana Sang, and Giang.

"Let's hope this doesn't take too long," he said.

"One way or another, the end is near," offered Hellman.

"Don't translate that, Giang," said Welch, shaking his head.

He watched as the line of soldiers in front of the boats scanned the group of Saigonese. He could see them assessing—the group had few possessions but surely there would be some money hidden somewhere, wouldn't there? The Nung guards, also sensing their interest, inched forward, and all guns were raised a little higher.

APRIL 30 — THE LAST DAY

The hours dragged by. It had been just after 10 p.m. when they'd reached the beach. At about 1 a.m., one House Seven senior staffer, moving very slowly, pulled out her South Vietnamese identification card and shifted it toward her mouth. Over the next several hours, she chewed it into obliteration, erasing her name, her photo, and the South Vietnamese flag forever. Her neighbors in the sand, seeing her precaution, quietly and carefully followed suit.

It wasn't until the light began to rise in the east that a break in the standoff came. Into the silence of the pre-dawn ripped the grinding whine of the camp's jeep engine. As it shot past the guard station, a staccato of shots reverberated through the air. Every guard and soldier on the beach raised his gun and clicked it into firing position. Welch felt the hair rise on the back of his neck.

The jeep careened to within feet of the group, spraying sand in a wide arc, and Jack Dobbs jumped out before it had fully come to a shuddering halt. A half-dozen Nung guards jumped off the back of the vehicle and, sizing up the situation, took up ranks with the group already standing watch.

"What the hell are you still doing on the beach?"

Dobbs sputtered. Welch stood, his legs almost buckling from the long night in a defensive crouch.

"Dammit, Jack, what the hell was that?"

Dobbs looked around, startled. "What?"

"Didn't you hear the shots? Don't you know you just almost started a firefight?" He indicated the raised weapons. Dobbs seemed to take in the situation for the first time. He looked back toward the kiosk and raised his hands in a conciliatory gesture. The two guards stared at him, the muzzles of their M-16s pointing right at him. Welch took a small step to one side.

"Sorry," he shouted. "Sorry, sorry, sorry."

The guards stared back sullenly but lowered their weapons, if only slightly. Dobbs turned back to Welch. "Works every time."

The tension in the air was still palpable. Welch decided not to pursue it; if no one had fired by now, they were probably safe for the moment. He looked at his people staring up at him. Their faces were taut with fear and anxiety.

"Look, Dobbs, we need your help," said Welch. "We're in a stalemate here, our guards against theirs. Can you get back in your jeep and go find Commander Dao and ask him to send the goddamned permission to get these two Mike boats off the beach and to the ship?"

"Sure, sure," said Dobbs, climbing back into the jeep.

"And, by the way, where the hell's the baggage?" Welch asked.

"It's still at the camp, loaded onto a flatbed truck. I

went back to the transmitter site and camp to check on the personnel we left," said Dobbs. "Those Vung Tau refugees they put into the camp north of us are all over the place, and word is there was a prison break. The situation's been getting worse by the hour."

The last words were a shout that floated out from the jeep. He was already heading out, picking up speed, oblivious to the guard's angry faces as he approached the kiosk. He held up one hand in a conciliatory gesture as he passed them.

Welch shook his head and yelled after him, "And don't forget the baggage!"

"It'll be a miracle if he doesn't get shot," said Hellman.

◆ ◆ ◆

It was a long three hours before Dobbs returned, this time stopping at the gate for a short chat with the guards there. As he approached the beach, the sound of his jeep caused all heads to turn, but while not one M-16 had been lowered while he'd been gone, nor one firing pin gently put back into place, there was no move to fire; everyone was weary. Welch's eyes were stinging from the effort of staying open. He rubbed them as he addressed Dobbs.

"Thanks for coming back, Jack. Please tell us you have good news."

"Thanh wasn't available," he said. "So I had a meeting with his assistant. I told him my problems, he told me his and, finally, when I agreed to stay with some of my men to assist him for a while after you take off, he signed the order for you all to get on your way."

He handed the order to Welch, who glanced at the Vietnamese writing and the red ink stamp. Giang took it from him and approached the South Vietnamese leader. When he saw the order, he shouted down the line and the soldiers lowered their guns and began to file away, all the menace gone from their faces. Now they were just tired men, hoping for a meal or some sleep or to see their loved ones before their uncertain end came upon them.

The decks of the Mike boats were already hot beneath their feet as the staggering House Seven group loaded onto them. Welch and Hellman looked at their wristwatches and exchanged a look. It was nearly 8:30

a.m. on April 30. They had missed the deadline for the evacuation of all Americans from Vietnam.

"We're going to make it," said Hellman. "Better late than never."

"Let's get to the ship first," said Welch, "then we'll celebrate. John must be wondering where the hell we are."

An hour later, as they approached the U.S. American Challenger—a truly welcome sight—the boat captain called the ship for loading instructions. Before long, he was snapping in frustration. Mr. Giang said there was some confusion, the Mike boat captain did not want to go around the ship, but to stay on the shore side. The crew of the Challenger was insisting that they head to starboard.

Mr. Giang's face was drawn. "He is threatening to return to shore."

"Good Lord," said Welch. "Offer him safe passage for him and his family if he just gets us onto that ship."

Giang translated and the boat captain nodded, but only begrudgingly passed the port side to make his way to starboard. The boarding took place, for the most part, without incident. One staffer lost a shoe as she climbed the rope ladder.

"My one shoe dropped," she said. "So I just kicked the other shoe after it. Because . . . what can you do with one shoe?"

◆ ◆ ◆

It wasn't until nearly 3 o'clock that afternoon that Dobbs and his men finally arrived at the ship. They came without the baggage. Despite Dobbs's efforts, Camp Seven had been raided by a mob of soldiers, prisoners, and refugees with machetes. Furious at being left behind to face the communists alone, they had hacked the evacuee's belongings to bits in a rage, destroying everything. Dobbs was chagrined at the loss but unapologetic.

Presidential orders telling Ambassador Graham Martin to get out of Saigon NOW.

"Well, damnation, if we'd been given water transport one day earlier this wouldn't have happened," he said. "We had only three goddamned boats—so it was either baggage and equipment or people. I was instructed to evacuate people, so I got people out."

"You did, indeed," said Welch. He clapped the

radio technician on the back. Now that they were all aboard, he couldn't keep the smile off his face. "You did indeed—we all did. And now you're here and we're on our way. It's too bad about the stuff—I mean, we must have less to our names now than the day we were born—but we got everyone out with their lives, and that's more than they could have expected had we stayed in Saigon. No one can complain about that."

♦ ♦ ♦

Big Minh's deadline for all representatives of the American government to be out of Vietnam had been the previous day, so Welch and Hellman were quite nearly the last two American evacuees to take their feet off Vietnamese soil, with Dobbs being the very last. All of them had overstayed the dubious welcome even longer than Ambassador Graham Martin, who had had to be plied from his office at 4:30 a.m. by a young helicopter pilot bearing a message scrawled on a notepad: "The President of the United States directs Ambassador Martin to come out to this helicopter."

Graham, who had been on the phone, trying, of all things, to get permission from Washington to extend the deadline for the evacuation, put down the receiver and followed the pilot to the waiting copter. Nearly three hours later, at 7:53 a.m., after lowering the American flag from atop the embassy, the last Marine Security Guards, narrowly evading enemy fire, finally lifted off the roof. Saigon had been cleared.

APRIL 30 — SUNSET

Now safely aboard the American Challenger, the House Seven employees looked back at the little island that had been their last refuge on Vietnamese soil. As the light began to fade from the sky, a huge plume of smoke rose over the site of their safe haven, "Camp Seven."

Whatever they had left behind was now completely destroyed, having been ransacked and set afire. It was almost too much to bear. Then, when the Vietnamese Beatles and the other singers raised their voices in a final farewell song, tears began to flow. The famous song, *Thuyen Vien Xu*, Boat Leaving, rose in waves while the sun set on a bittersweet day. They had made it out safely, but the land to which they had belonged was no longer theirs to call home.

MAY 1 – 6

The American Challenger did not leave the waters off of Phu Quoc until mid-morning on May 1. The relief of escape and the sadness at leaving was soon to be overshadowed by the stress of survival at sea.

The ship steamed east and then south, making good speed at about 20 knots. As it passed the small island of Con Son off the Mekong Delta, all eyes turned to watch the receding green dot disappear into the vast blue sea. It would be their last view of Vietnam for a long, long time, if not forever.

The rendezvous of the entire evacuation fleet took place about 60 miles southeast of Vung Tau. It was the largest such gathering of ships that Welch had ever heard of. There were two or three carriers, several destroyers, multiple supply ships, and at least four freighters also laden with refugees. Choppers flew between them, criss-crossing in mid-air as they transferred supplies and personnel. Small boats also continually arrived throughout the day, so overladen with desperate refugees that it was a miracle they were still afloat.

Orders came in that the American Challenger was to take on nearly 4,000 more refugees—"a motley crew of fishermen and villagers plus two-time refugees from Cam Ranh." The water was rougher than just off of Phu

Quoc, and the transfer was not as smooth. Onlookers gasped as one woman slipped from high on the rope ladder and plunged, arms flailing, into the sea far below. After some struggle, she was rescued by the crew. Those watching cheered despite the fact that she would be one more person jockeying for space on the crowded deck.

The transfer of refugees took until well past midnight on May 2. Welch captured the images on a tiny Page-A-Day Calendar:

> Thursday, May 1 Challenger weighed anchor at 10am after rendezvous with Dubuque for supplies just outside of the 3-mile limit. Took on refugees here – some frightful sights.

> Common kitchens set up and our people got short shrift by swarming refugees . . . Unfortunately they mixed in with our embassy people. Altogether 5,029 Vietnamese aboard.

Early that morning, as the Challenger began to steam east in a convoy with two other freighters and two US Navy destroyers, James Welch managed to get a telegram off to his wife back in Boise, Idaho. It was the first she'd heard from him since he'd dashed off that quick letter on April 21, a period of nearly two weeks:

> Am aboard American Challenger with all my people bound for Guam. Doing OK. Love, Jim.

Halfway through the trip, on May 3, despite the many rumors, the ship did not put into the Naval Base at Subic Bay. The refugee camps in the Philippines were already filled to capacity, and the weary travelers were ordered to proceed to Guam. It would be another three long days on deck. By day, the sun beat down mercilessly onto the ship, but by evening, it could become chilly, and on some nights, heavy rains and wind pummeled the group.

The additional refugees warmed the House Seven living spaces and common kitchens, turning the remnants of "Camp Seven" into a muddled free-for-all. The makeshift dispensary was trying to serve all 5,000 Vietnamese aboard, stretching provisions to the limits. Supplies and treatment for pink eye, diarrhea, rashes, and fevers were beginning to run low. People were tiring of lining up to receive their meals from the large cauldrons on

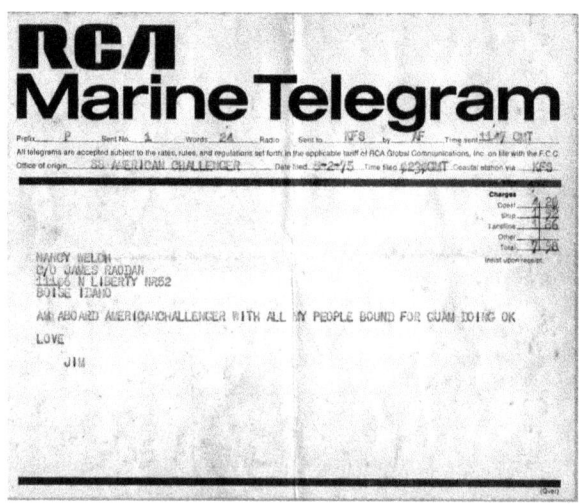

This May 2, 1975 telegram was the first news home in nearly two weeks.

deck; the watered-down rice gruel with flecks of boiled chicken, onions, and carrots was no longer appetizing and barely fortifying.

Welch continued to meet daily with the community leaders who had been appointed on Phu Quoc to hear these types of complaints and to pass out whatever instructions he had. He and Hana Sang remained close, though under the eyes of the captain and the Marines, they could not spend as much time together as they had on Phu Quoc.

However, since most people still came to her with their problems and fears—and that was obvious to all—they still spent hours a day talking on deck under the open sky, her skin turning dark, Welch's red, then deeply freckled. He could not help but find her presence soothing. No matter the upset among the staff members, she was the voice of calm and reason. Once she became involved in any situation, tempers calmed, fears were allayed, anxieties soothed.

He counted his blessings again and again that she had stuck with him, with the evacuation; she could have chosen to leave earlier with her family, who had made their way safely to Paris before Tan Son Nhut was bombed. One evening, hoping to provide her with a treat and some relief from the routine on deck, he visited the ship's galley and helped himself to the food on the stove. He later learned that it was the captain's supper, "which caused something of a stir. End of that routine," he wrote to his wife.

The final days on the Challenger dragged, the sea and sky an unchanging blue all around them. They could not help but spend their time wondering what the next step would bring. Welch hoped it would be an easing of the hardships his people faced, but feared that, once they arrived on Guam, they would be lost among the tens of thousands of refugees who were also descending on the small island. While it would be a relief to get to shore, he knew that the journey toward a new life—and the process of making a new home— promised to be a long one.

He tried not to think about the day he would have to return to his normal life. There would certainly be a debriefing in Washington—would he be seen as a hero or an insubordinate? He had not been responsible for the fall of Vietnam, but he felt like he might as well be blamed. All the work he so strongly believed in had come to nothing in the end. Or worse than nothing? As he looked out upon the nearly 1,000 people he had provided safe passage for, he could not foresee what was in store for them. He believed deep in his heart that it had to be better than living under communist rule, but how much better?

He tried not to think, either, about the coming separation from Hana Sang. They were now an indisputable team, bonded by common purpose. His American home, his American family, seemed as distant and unreal at this moment as the future of the refugees. How, after all that he had just been through, would he

This front page of a Guam newspaper captured the staggering plight of the refugees. My father's ship, the American Challenger, arrived just before the ship pictured here, but the scene was much the same.

return to meals at McDonald's, managing affairs with an understandably traumatized wife, and trying to be a loving father to seven kids?

Welch looked to the eastern horizon, where all that future lay just over the curve of the Earth. The future would come, as it always did, without promises, but with possibilities. Certainly with possibilities.

15,000 Arrive Here Ragged And Dazed

By Jim Eggensperger
City Editor

Barefoot and ragged, bewildered and dazed, 15,000 refugees landed here yesterday on three cargo ships.

They held their entire worlds in plastic or paper sacks, bags of all descriptions or the big tin cans used by cafeterias.

In contrast to evacuees who flew here earlier in Operation New Life, the South Vietnamese arriving at Naval Station's Sierra Pier carried few personal effects, little money, and most could not answer the question: "Do you speak English?"

They had been crowded on the docks and into the holds of three U.S. Lines cargo carriers, the American Challenger, the Pioneer Commander and the Pioneer Contender.

An eyewitness who rode one of the ships from the breakwater at Apra Harbor to the pier said the ship carried a "strong odor of urine and body odor."

U.S. Marines aboard the ship had built privies onto the edges of the deck so that offal went directly into the ocean.

The eyewitness said the deck appeared to be "wet and slimy."

A Protestant minister who arrived on the first ship to dock, the American Challenger, said he found it difficult to sleep because "much people, much people, much people."

The minister, Nguyen Liam An, said he had been picked up by the ship on Phone Quoc

Both the upper and lower decks of the Pioneer Commander, the second ship to arrive yesterday, contained huge crowds of Vietnamese refugees anxious to disembark. Daily News photographer P.J. Ryan rode into the dock aboard the ship.

clothing. Very cold. And the the mobile Hilton Far East. Refugees who has been sailing presented no danger to the

PAGE ONE—TUESDAY, APRIL 29

Capt. Thien put his family aboard Challenger causing some panic on base and general alarm which put all vessels to sea without lights. Also caused us to disembark after loading 2 Mike boats. Much tension because of menacing naval guards with M-16s facing our Nungs also with M-16s. Bowman, Thinh and I were also armed with handguns. Tension grew when Gass' jeep was fired on for not stopping at Base and all M-16's were clicked into firing position. Our 250 people were well disciplined and I had all the heads down and gun drawn to put out spotlights if necessary. Earlier 2-5 (?) truck convoys had taken us to debarkation point at 10pm – 2 hours late. Much sweat over that. All bags are put in warehouse.

Tuesday, April 29

8.00	Capt Thien put his family
8.30	aboard Challenger causing
9.00	some panic on base + genl alarm
9.30	which put all vessels to sea
10.00	without lights. Also caused
10.30	us to disembark after loading
11.00	2 Mike boats. Much tension
11.30	because of menacing naval
NOON	guards with M-16s facing our
1.00	Nungs also with M-16. Bowman,
1.30	Thinh and I were also armed with

PAGE TWO—WEDNESDAY, APRIL 30

Boarded American Challenger after harrowing night waiting
to board Mike (LSM-8) boats. Guarded well by Nungs (?) from
Saigon and reinforced by Nungs from Rach Gia in early morning. Boarded about 0830 and boarded Challenger without incident 1 hour later. Slight scare when Mike crew and Challenger
differed on which side of ship to board. Some feared we would
put back to shore. But he was finally persuaded and hauled into
starboard. Gass joined us in the PM and we learned the fate of
our baggage – all lost due to vandalism by the soldiers, prisoners and refugees. About 100 Navy family including Cmdr Tho,
Deputy of Base, Navy crews abandoned boats.

Wednesday, April 30

8.00	NOTES
8.30	Boarded American Challenger
9.00	after harrowing night waiting
9.30	to board Mike (LSM-8) boats.
10.00	Guarded well by Nungs from Saigon
10.30	+ reinforced by Nungs from Rach
11.00	Gia in early morning. Boarded
11.30	about 0830 and boarded Challenger
NOON	without incident 1 hr. later. Slight
1.00	scare when Mike crew and
1.30	Challenger crew differed on which
2.00	

THU BA
TUESDAY
MARDI

29

18 tháng 3

APRIL
1975

Su Mo Tu We Th Fr Sa
1 2 3 4 5
6 7 8 9 10 11 12
13 14 15 16 17 18 19
20 21 22 23 24 25 26
27 28 29 30

225

PAGE THREE—THURSDAY, MAY 1

Challenger weighed anchor at 10am after taking aboard to rendezvous with Dubuque for supplies just outside of 3-mile limit. [something scratched out: 3600 refugees – a motley crew of fishermen and villages plus 2-time refugees from Cam Ranh.] Unfortunately they mixed in with our embassy people. Much jockeying for places on deck. C-rations distributed. I got our doctors and nurses together and with Capt. M. Mallick, head of Marine contingent, moved to set up makeshift dispensary. Altogether 5,029 Vietnamese aboard.

Movement of our ship caused 55 Rincon to head to sea and caused panic on shore

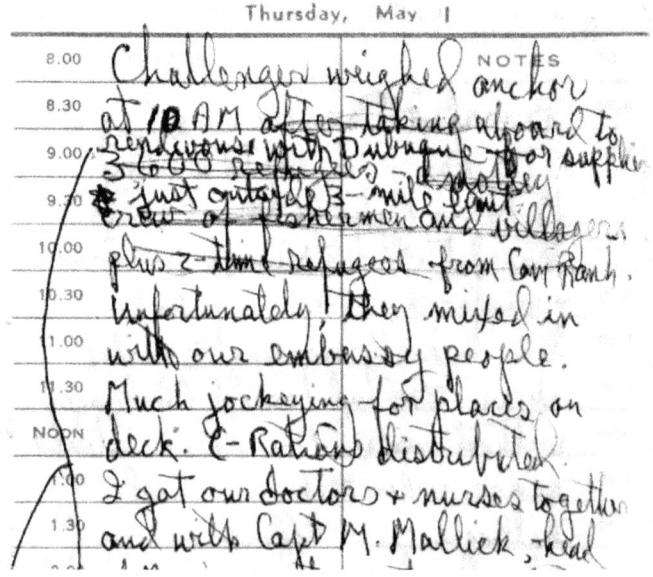

PAGE FOUR—FRIDAY, MAY 2

Steamed east and south around Delta. Guam announced as destination with stop for supplies at holding area in S. China Sea (Challenger is 21,000 DW ton freighter out of N.Y. capable of 22 knots) We are steaming at 19-21 knots. Reached holding area after passing Con Son – last view of VN. Received supplies by chopper. Never seen such a large sea rendezvous. 2-3 carriers, several destroyers, supply ships and at least four freighters with refugees. Choppers flying between each of them.

Took on refugees here – some frightful sights including one woman plunging into the sea who was rescued. Common kitchens set up and our people got short shrift by swarming refugees. [end of page]

	Friday, May 2	THU NAM THURSDAY JEUDI
8.00	NOTES	
8.30	Steamed east & South around	
9.00	Delta. Guam announced as	
9.30	destination with stop for supplies	
10.00	at holding area in S. China Sea	
10.30	(Challenger) is 21,000 DW ton freighter	20 tháng 5
11.00	out of N.Y. capable of 22 knots) We	
11.30	are steaming at 19-21 knots. Reached	MAY 1975
NOON	holding area after passing Con	
1.00	Son - last view of VN. Received	Su Mo Tu We Th Fr Sa 1 2 3
1.30	supplies by chopper. Never seen	4 5 6 7 8 9 10 11 12 13 14 15 16 17 18 19 20 21 22 23 24

PAGE FIVE—SATURDAY, MAY 3

Steamed East toward Philippines. Whole day was filled [with] rumors and speculations about putting into Subic Bay. Last decision, just ½ hour before time to go into Subic was to head for Guam. Crew disappointed—they wanted mail & shore leave. We also hoped for word of Jones, Hai & Hong as well as LST 504-505 from Vung Tau with 3 husbands of our women passengers & equipment. Feeding system improved but people do not take well to fare of sticky rice or gruel with chicken and onions/carrots from ....boxes ?. Dispensary very busy with pink eye, diarrhea, rashes, fevers. Got Mai Lan some chow from the galley and later learned it was the Capts supper. End of that routine.

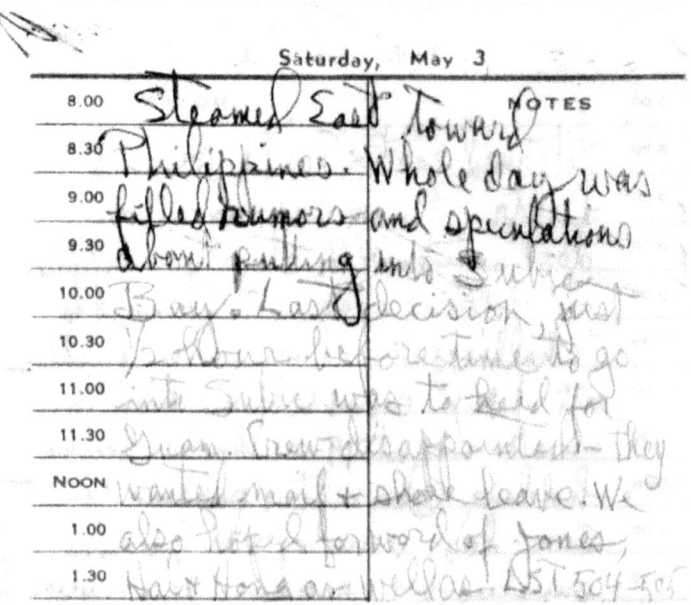

PAGE FOUR—SUNDAY, MAY 4

Only 3 more days. What will the next step bring? An easing of
the hardships for the people, I hope but I fear being inundated
by 10s of thousands of refugees. Losing track of all time, we had
a problem determining what day it is. (All foregoing from 29
April written today)

Heavy rains and wind last night hard on people on deck.

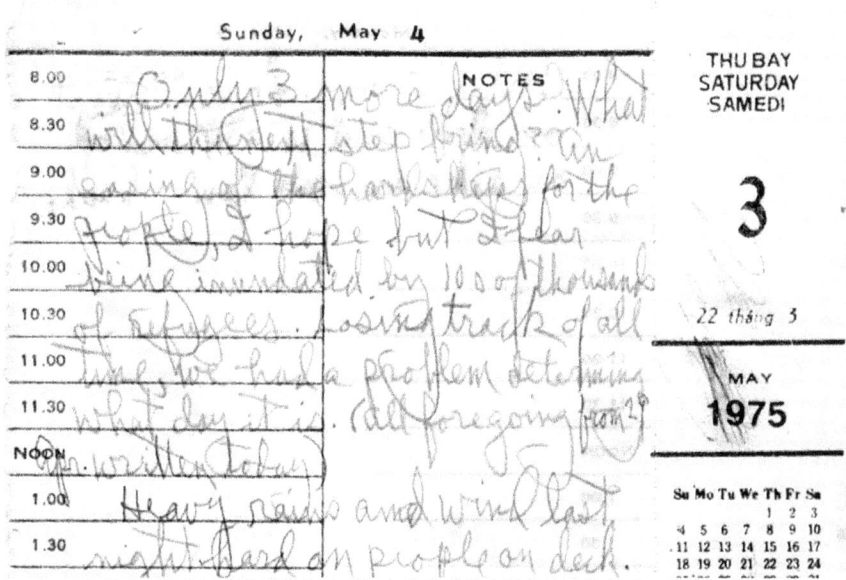

PAGE FIVE—MONDAY, MAY 5

Only 2 more days. Slept on deck and it got rid of an ache in my lower back.

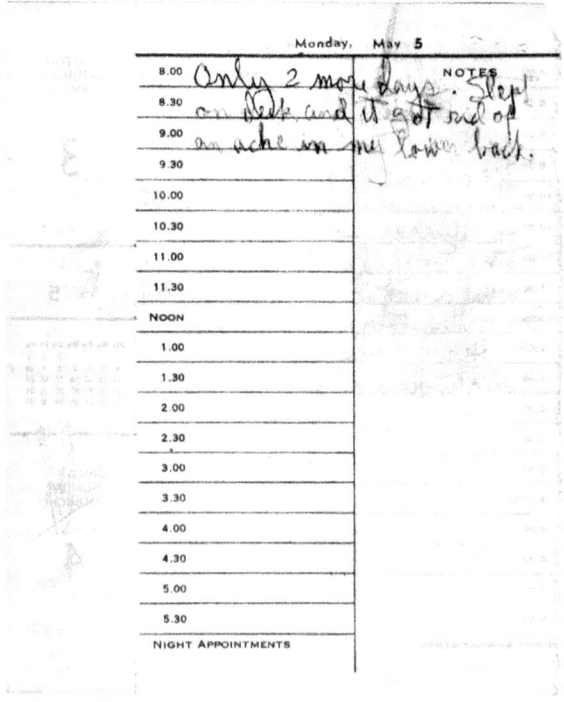

WITH LOVE FROM THE CHALLENGER
— THE FULL LETTER

MY FATHER WROTE THIS LETTER TO US FIVE DAYS AFTER ESCAPING FROM VIETNAM.

American Challenger
Approx, 40 mi. E. of Philippines
5 May 1975

Dear Nance, troops and Rabs [grandparents],

I am sitting in an upper deck cabin looking out the porthole at booms and rigging of this 21,000 ton freighter. Below all these wires and steel are 5,029 [or is it 5,009] refugees not counting us four Americans—Bowman, Taber, Gass and me. Jones never made it out of Saigon in time to join us. TSN [Tan Son Nhut Airport] was bombed, rocketed and closed the night before he was to come. The irony was that the day before, Monday, an empty C-46 arrived in Phu Quoc with only 2 cases of brandy aboard. Jones, Hai and a few others should have been on that flight. I assume Jones made it by chopper to the fleet or Subic Bay, but I fear for Mr. Hai.

Our group consists of something like 935 people connected with the [CIA] project and other embassy activities and the story of our odyssey and exodus would rank with some of the better fiction of that type if it were put into the right shape. Briefly, as I saw what [the] declining moral in ARVN pulling out of northern positions without a fight, public order disintegrating, and the results of panic were doing in Danang,

Dear Nance, troops and Rabs,

    I am sitting in an upper deck cabin looing out the porthole at booms and rigging of this 21,000 ton freighter. Below all these wires and steel are 5,029 refugees not counting us four Americans--Bowman, Taber, Gass and me. Jones never made it out of Saigon in time to join us. TSN was bombed, rocketed and closed the night before he was to come. The irony was that the day before, Monday, an empty C-46 arrived in Phu Quoc with only 2 cases of brandy aboard. Jones, Hai and a few others should have been on that flight.

Nha Trang and Cam Ranh I began to send priority traffic to Washington to get my group out yesterday. I could never bring them together in the midst of Saigon's millions with curfews and panic. In quick order we considered Vung Tau, Phu Quoc and tiny Phu Qui Island as places to relocate and start our Station anew (we never dreamed that events would unfold as fast as they did). Transmitters and all of House #7 equipment and furniture was packed and we finally settled on Phu Quoc as most secure. I made an exploratory trip there with Bowman and Gass and came up with an abandoned Vietnam MP Battalion HQ. It took a few days for top Vietnam clearance and meantime we were underway shipping stuff so that when the clearance came we were already moving. I had gone through the paces of evacuation with my people for weeks so they were very well disciplined. Air America mounted a massive airlift of over 800 people for us in 3 days plus extra flights for food and some equipment like jeeps and telex machines. Everything seemed to come except our personal [items] so we spent several days without a change of clothes or adequate washing facilities. I told Hal and Charlie I had never been so dirty for so long and I guess it's true. We were at the Phu Quoc camp about 8 days and, like in a kibbutz, starting from nothing except bare buildings, we had a fairly comfortable set up by the end even though we were for the most part still sleeping on mats on the floor.

When Bien Hoa was closed and Vung Tau taken it was obvious the game was up and any thought of reestablishing the station [was given up]. "Mother" was closed down and I turned my attention to making an evacuation plan. You have to know the geography of the Southern tip of the island to understand it but mainly I wanted to avoid passing through town and panic all the people there by using the back bay. It never came off. We made our exit in five Navy trucks after curfew. Charlie escorted the first group of about 600 and got directly to the ship (how we got to the ship is another story); about 250 followed to be taken by two smaller landing craft were accompanied by Hal, Mai Lan and me due to a combination of bureaucratic and "panic" circumstances we didn't make it that night and spend the entire night huddled before the ramps of the landing craft in the fear that there would be a shoot-out between our Nung guards and the edgy Navy security types who obviously resented two Americans and their Saigonese leaving when they couldn't. A lot of that came after we finally left the next morning.

The deadline for all Americans out of Vietnam was the previous noon so we were presumably about the last Americans out of [the] country with Don Gass possibly the last. He was to return with trucks for our baggage from soldiers, prisoners from a nearby camp and refugees had already gone amok and were hacking it all to pieces with machetes. So we lost almost everything. As did many others, I had only the clothes on my back—a blue shirt and my gray Levis cut off to make shorts. So now I presumably have less than I did when I was born.

I particularly regret the loss of my elephant hide bag, the tan calfskin carryall, my typewriter, camera, Chris' radio, not to speak of clothes. Your small gray suitcase and square tri-taper cosmetic bag were there too. Probably someday I can make a claim but I'll have to do some shopping in Guam to get presentable clothes. I now am wearing a pair of dungarees I bought from the ship's store. I regret the loss of everybody's property—but we did get them out alive which more than I would have been able to say had we remained in Saigon.

The lot of the evacuees (mine) and the refugees on the Challenger is not a happy one. They are all crowded together on the decks and in holds, food is unappetizing—C-rations before and now we have batches of rice with some chicken and onions thrown in, water at a common watering spot. Diarrhea, pinkeye and fevers are prevalent. But we brought four doctors and three nurses with us to Phu Quoc whom I have put at the disposal of the ship and a makeshift dispensary is running round the clock. I still have morning meetings with Mr. Thinh, my assistant, and Mr. Chuc, the elected head of our Vietnamese community in Phu Quoc to pass out whatever instructions I have and to learn their problems. I also meet with Mai Lan on the other side of the ship for the same reasons since most people come to her with their problems and fears. She has been great. She stuck by my side when she could have remained or gone back to accompany her family to safety and ease in NY or Paris. The two younger kids did go back and I learned by radio that they were successfully evacuated with her parents a few days before TSN was closed. I have tried to bring Mai Lan over everyday for a shower and some warm food but it is kind of dicey because of the strict Marine security and last night it seems I inadvertently took the Captain's supper which caused something of a stir. Oh well! Someday I will have to write a book.

That is about all for now. Will mail this and call from Guam. I probably will stay with the group until it reaches the States and then we can make some plans.

This has been a unique experience but not one I would want to repeat.

Love to all, Jim / Dad

EPILOGUE

My father and his people alighted on the small American territory of Guam in the dark of night on May 6. It was not until early the next morning, when everyone was off the ship and into the refugee processing system, that he, Bowman, Gass, and Taber were finally able to find a room at the Cliff Hotel in downtown Agana and collapse onto their beds, sixteen grueling days after leaving Saigon.

Gass took off directly for home, Taber was quickly reassigned to the CIA Station in Taiwan, and my father and Bowman stayed on to help the agency team that had been sent to take on the responsibility of processing visa paperwork for the House Seven evacuees.

Undoubtedly, Mai Lan and my father kept up their close their close friendship, both out of affection for each other and so that she could facilitate the work of communicating with and reassuring the families who were one step closer to freedom but still without any road map or guarantees.

On June 2, my father joined us in Idaho, where we'd finished the school year, and the nine of us set out for a cross-country car ride back to D.C. Our first stop was Boulder, Colorado, to visit our father's sister, Jean Williams. She was only too happy to see him but said that from the moment she laid eyes on him, she knew that he was forever changed.

"He was a broken man. I could just tell," she said. "He thought he had lost the war all on his own."

By the end of 1975, my mother would write that he was not so uptight anymore, no longer "crying out in his sleep."

In the same letter, she spoke of being proud to bring the four oldest kids—Michelle, Chris, Mike, and John—to a special ceremony where my father was given a Certificate of Distinction from CIA director William E. Colby:

To James Welch — with thanks and best wishes — WEColly   18 Dec 75

In recognition of his sustained superior performance under hazardous conditions from March through May 1975 in South Vietnam. Mr. Welch played a key role as a member of a small team which continued a radio operation under conditions of increasing adversity and later arranged the successful evacuation of the team's Vietnamese associates. Mr. Welch's flexibility, imagination, determination and demonstrated courage were in the finest traditions of the service, reflecting credit on him and the Central Intelligence Agency.

Still—though I never heard him say it—he must have been all too aware there was so much that was left undone. In the following months, my parents received many letters from the House Seven employees, expressing thanks and affection. Some were also seeking help, as they had been dropped into a foreign land with little by way of guidance and assistance, despite the sponsorship program that provided them American families to rely on. Indeed, many had not received their final weeks' pay and all needed employment—some asked directly for help finding jobs, others for recommendations, some just for goodwill and prayers. Though he did what he could, it could not have been easy to come to terms with the fact that though he had facilitated their way out of communist hands, the journey of setting up a new life in America was not one he could accompany them on.

In 1976, at the age of 52, and in the throes of trying to decide whether he should stay with the agency

CIA Director William Colby presenting the post-evacuation Certificate of Distinction. He later matted and personally signed: To James Welch, with thanks and best wishes, W.E. Colby, 18 Dec 1975.

or retire, my father made an uncharacteristic move and called his sister to ask her advice: Should he take another assignment from the agency?

"I don't know why he asked me; he never asked me such things," she said. "But I think he was just done. I said, 'No, Jim, you've done all you can.' And he put in his resignation."

I can't help but think there was some pressure from my mother as well. She orchestrated a greeting card coup to get most of us kids to congratulate him on his good decision to retire and move on out to the balmy climes of Hawaii.

And so it was that he retired in August 1976, after 27 years in the service of his country as part of the Central Intelligence Agency. That October the nine of us moved to Hawaii, which, for my mother at least, was the perfect setting to live both with the comfort and security of America and the multiculturalism she had become accustomed to living in the Far East.

It was the first time in six years that she could set up a household and not have to worry about moving—or evacuating it—at the whim of outside forces.

◆ ◆ ◆

My father died in October 1992, just 16 years after the fall of South Vietnam, at the age of 67. Fifteen years after his death, in an amazing coincidence, my brother Chris ran into the daughter of a House Seven employee at a Christmas party. She told him that her father had

never let the family forget what Mr. James E. Welch
had done for them, and how he had kept a photo of our
family on a shelf in their living room.

"My father would take your picture down all the
time," she said. "He would point out your father and
tell us all your names. We knew of you all through our
childhood. He really respected your father and valued
his friendship. He was very kind, and was not just using
the Vietnamese for workers."

My father went to Vietnam thinking to be a force
for good, thinking to hold back the tide of communism and of tyranny. In the process, he fell in love with
Vietnam and with its people. But in the end, the U.S.
involvement was nothing short of disastrous. He never
truly shook off the burden of that incongruity. However,
in his final days, he was given one sweet reminder of
what he had done for so many people in those final days
of April 1975.

In 1992, he left Maui to seek treatment in Southern
California for his terminal medical condition. During
the admittance process, the intake doctor, a young res-
ident, took one look at the name on his clipboard and
gasped in surprise.

"Mr. Welch?!" he said. He looked from the page to
his patient in the wheelchair and back again. He could
not stop repeating the name. "Mr. Welch? Mr. Welch?
James Welch?"

My father looked at the bright Vietnamese face and
the truth dawned on him.

"Were you on the American Challenger?" he asked.

"Yes, I was," the doctor said. "My family was—you saved our lives."

My father extended his hand and the young doctor took it and shook it over and over again.

"Mr. Welch," he repeated. "Mr. Welch."

"Well, isn't this fantastic," said my father, holding the doctor's hand with both of his, tears forming in the corners of his eyes. "Isn't this just fantastic."

James E. Welch, December 26, 1924-October 17, 1992

"Thumbs up, Old Soldier"

~ *from eulogy by his sister Jean Williams*

APPENDICES

KAT FITZPATRICK TIMELINE

1966	Born Fairfax, Virginia
1970-72	Lived in Korea
1972-74	Lived in Taiwan (while father worked in VN)
July 6, 1974	April 1975 – Moved to Saigon
April 3, 1975	Fled from Saigon
June 1975	Returned to D.C.
1976-2000	Primarily resided on Maui
2000-2012	Primarily resided in Upstate New York
2012	Decision to write about Vietnam
2013	Enrolled in MFA program
2015	Traveled to Vietnam to retrace father's final days in Saigon and Phu Quoc
2015	Published *The Fight to Write*
2016	Graduated with a Masters in Fine Arts in Creative Writing
2016-2021	Balanced full-time work with writing and the coronavirus pandemic
2022	Vietnam presentation at The Paine Castle in Troy, N.Y. (See tinyurl.com/Kat-Fitzpatrick-Vietnam)
2023	First edition of "For the Love of Vietnam" published

THE VIETNAM ERA: A BRIEF TIMELINE

Tonkin Gulf Incident	August 2, 1964
The first U.S. combat troops arrive	March 1965
The North Vietnamese launch the Tet (Lunar New Year) Offensive, which is televised widely in the U.S.	January 1968
U.S. troop numbers in Vietnam reach 540,000	December 1968
President Richard Nixon orders the first of many troop withdrawals from Vietnam	July 1969
James E. Welch is transferred to the Saigon CIA Station	September 1972
The Paris Peace Accords are signed, providing a cease-fire	January 27, 1973
The last U.S. troops are withdrawn from Vietnam	March 29, 1973
Vietnam is opened up for American dependents to take residence	1974
The Welch family relocates from Taiwan to Vietnam	July 1974
Nixon resigns	August 9, 1974
The North Vietnamese Army launches a massive assault on South Vietnam	1975 March
The Welch family flies out	April 3
The Operation Babylift orphan evacuation plane crashes	April 4
All Americans are ordered to leave the country within 24 hours	April 28
Ambassador Graham Martin finally leaves Saigon	April 30, 4:58 a.m.
The last Marine Security Guards are rescued off the U.S. embassy roof	April 30, 7:53 a.m.
James Welch and his staff leave Phu Quoc Island via boat	April 30, 8:30 a.m.

A "Good Luck" Letter

March 16, 2005

Dear Chris,

I am sending this letter to you as I promised.

I did tell you the whole story about your father and his brave secret activities as boss of the famous "House Number 7" which CIA agent F. Snepp has mentioned in his book [Decent Interval] printed in America two decades ago.

One thing I wouldn't never (sic) forget your father was the moment of pandemonium of the fall of Saigon, in the radio room at Phu Quoc island, we received the ultimate message from the US Embassy: "Go and Good Luck!"

Your father held my hand and said, "Well, let's go Phien!" Then he quietly smiled and added: "I hope luck is with us!"

Instead of flying out of Viet Nam to Bangkok or to the 6th Fleet anchored nearby the South VN waters–your father chose the risk of sticking with his collaborators until all of them were safe in the American rescue boat. Now, hundreds of them and their families can breathe the air of freedom in America, and

all of them still keep in their heart the image and memory of their late great boss named Jim Welch, your father.

Best wishes to you and your family,
Phien Nguyen
Author,
Harrisburg, PA

Dear Chris,

I'm sending this document to you as I promised you.

I did tell you the whole story about your father and his brave secret activities as boss of the famous "House Number 7" which C.I.A. agent F. Snepp has had mentioned in his book printed in America 2 decades ago.

One thing I wouldn't never forget your father was the moment of pandemonium of the fall of Saigon, in the radio room at Phu Quốc island, we received the ultimate message from the US Embassy : « Go and Good luck » your father held my hand and said : « Well, let's go Phien ! » then he quietly smiled and added : « I hope luck is with us ! »

Instead of flying out of Vietnam — to Bangkok or to the 6th fleet anchored nearby the South VN water — your father has chosen the risk to stick with his collaborators until all of them were safe in the American rescue boat.

Now, hundred of them and their families can breath the air of freedom in America, and all of them still keep in their heart the image and memory of their late great boss named Jim Welch, your father.

Best wishes to you & your family

Phien Nguyen

PHIEN VAN NGUYEN
Author

Harrisburg, PA. 2005

April 18, 1975
519 Kukuau Street
Hilo, Hawaii   96720

welsch
Dear Mr. ~~Welsch~~, Mr. Bauman and Mr. Jones,

Just a few lines to let you know I have arrived in Hawaii
safely. I want all of you to know I greatly appreciate your
assistance in sending me to Hawaii. My father sends his thanks
and appreciation to you for helping me. He was surprised to learn
that Mr. Bauman was one of my bosses!

It is strange not to be at work, but I am also happy to be
with my family again. It's sure different after being in a scorching
sunshine and 24 hours later being in a chilly blue Hawaiian weather!
Please say hello to all my colleagues for me. I felt very sad
leaving them I hope everything goes well with them.

Again, thank you so much for your help. I also want to thank
you for helping my two friends 3. Demetria and Hoa. We all think
of the Americans that are left behind to help on the evacuation
job. I know it is an enormous job and we pray that your job
or rather plan will be successful. Thank you again.

Sincerely yours,

Theresa Quang

*I am deeply grateful to all of you for helping my daughter
while she was in Vietnam and for returning her safely to
me in Hawaii. I am proud to have been a member of your
professional and dedicated organization. My deepest gratitude
also to Bear Cox.
Aloha, and get out safe!*

George MORTON

This is one happy letter that details a successful escape.
This letter of thanks to my father and his colleagues was
written just two weeks just before the Fall of Saigon.

5317 BRILEY PLACE
WASHINGTON, D. C. 20016

July 28, 1976

Mr. James E. Welch
11106 Redford Court
Fairfax, Virginia 22030

Dear Jim:

Thank you so much for your thoughtful letter of
July 17th. My very best wishes to you on your retirement, which I hope brings you all the satisfaction you
deserve from your fine work for the Agency over these
years.

Please give my very sincere best wishes to Theresa
Quang and to George Morton. I was particularly concerned at Theresa's situation in Saigon in the last
days, and I am delighted to thank you personally for
the extra effort I am sure you took on her behalf. I
thought the Station and you who worked with her helped
her as much as possible in finding meaningful and sub-
stantial work and of course also in ensuring her safety
in the last period.

Thanks again for everything you have done for her,
for me, for the Agency, and for your country.

Sincerely,

W. E. Colby

Upon his retirement in 1976, my father wrote a letter of
good-bye and thanks to the then-director of the CIA,
William Colby. He received this reply in return.

LOSING ANNA

The following series of letters was included in my parents' papers. They tell a story which does not need much embellishment, but they, of themselves, depict one sliver of the often unseen (by us in America) effects of the war. Unlike Theresa Quang's story depicted on the prior pages, this one has no tidy resolution.

A reminder: my family left Saigon on April 3rd and my father was busy with the crush of the invasion and evacuation. He may have forwarded the letters on to my mother as it appears that she responded from Boise before Grant's final letter of May 5, 1975.

◆ ◆ ◆

APRIL 2, 1975

Dear Mrs. Welch –

I have today forwarded a package via parcel post addressed to you, but which is actually intended for Miss Anna Tran Thi Doa ... a clerk in a dress shop in Saigon and we understand that both of you are somewhat acquainted.

I must apologize to you for taking this liberty and then asking that you deliver the parcel to Miss Anna, but in the interest of saving time during unknown conditions recently I thought this might be the best way...

Mrs. Welch, we people back here cannot know fully what you may be going through in Saigon today but please know that our prayers and hopes are constantly for your safety and also for the safety especially for those in Vietnam whom we also know.

Our family has for some years corresponded with Anna and her friends and we cannot bear to think of her and her family being burdened with more problems and trouble. We love her very much.

Thank you, Mrs. Welch, for assisting us in getting this parcel to Anna.

Sincerely,

Mr. and Mrs. Ralph S.
and son, Grant S.

◆ ◆ ◆

APRIL 3, 1975

Dear Mr & Mrs. Welch,

You must surely be tiring of me by this time, but must do whatever I can for Anna. What we (my parents and I) are now doing is trying to arrange for Anna's sister, Luu, to come over here immediately on a visitor's visa. Immigrations says it's fairly easy to do, and later when the Saigon Gov't falls, she will simply be declared a refugee. At least will have her here at that time. We'll also try to find others to do the same for the other three as soon as possible, but no guarantees.

In a few days you should receive a letter from my parents which will contain a typed letter for Luu inviting her to visit them in California for as long as possible. There may also be a financial affidavit and an airline ticket, but we may have Pan Am reserve the ticket for her to pick up at the Pan Am window at the airport instead of mailing it. It will be paid in cash here. With the letter, etc. she should have no trouble in obtaining the visa and getting out of there very soon. Again, thanks for everything.

Sincerely,
Grant

◆ ◆ ◆

APRIL 5, 1975

Mrs. Welch,

This note to you is written very hurriedly as time today seems to be of the essence, and I know you will understand.

In our hasty attempt to get Luu (Tranthe Luu), sister of Anna, over here on even so much as a Visitor visa we encounter so much detail and red-tape over the the usual procedures that we are attempting every short-cut we can muster, even to Mr. Ford, to approve some instant way to do this.

Enclosed is a copy of the letter which is on its way to Luu but that is in the usual procedure. Mrs. Shroyer and myself spent yesterday with Immigration in San Diego to little avail as they are under so much pressure. We are now working to have Congressman Clair W. Burgener (San Diego) in Washington, DC do what he can.

Our son, Grant, is again writing to you today. I am preparing Support Affidavits to use if required in this "instant" solution.

Hastily, with apologies to you and thanks to you.
Ralph S.

◆ ◆ ◆

APRIL 14, 1975

Dear Mrs. Welch,

I was very happy to write this short letter to you. I hear you and your children return home alright. I call your home in Saigon and we know you be fine. Please tell me how you are now. Today I didn't hear anything about my parents in Danang. I only pray for they safety.

And I will tell you the news from my sister who will go to U.S. soon if she get visa early. Mr. Ralph who is Grant father, he do very big help us but I know you are leaving Saigon. I will try very hard for this and will send my sister over there.

I knew you very kindness with me since you been in Saigon. And I am and my Luu sister never forget you kind. I start to do the visitor visa for Luu today but I don't know when she ready for you. I know many trouble in my country.

Please say hello to your children for me. Best wishes to you and your family. Thank you for everything again.

Sincerely,
Anna

◆ ◆ ◆

APRIL 23, 1975

Dear Welch,

I was very happy to write for you today. How are you and your children now? Did they go to school yet? How is the weather over there. I still work with Alice. I've many American friends go home. Maybe have a chance soon in Saigon.

I did not hear anything from my family. Last week my sister have airline ticket from Grant's parents, I hope my sister can leave Vietnam soon. I try to get out here too but I know very hard. Yesterday, I came to your house in Saigon for see your husband but he not there. Did he return home or still in Saigon? If he still here you please help me ask him for me, did my box from Grant parents come yet? and please let me know by my phone ... or my address ...

Dear Welch, please give me your favor. And now your husband very busy in his work but I don't know how get the things for supply. Please understand for me. We never forget your kindness with us since you been Saigon.

I hope someday I can get out this country. I will come to visit your family in U.S.A. We have more trouble around Saigon too. Everyone in the world very worried for Vietnam in future. I pray for the Peace come soon. Will write for you more if I have some news from my sister who try go to American. Please write for me soon if you can. Thank you again.

Sincerely,
Anna

◆ ◆ ◆

MAY 4, 1975

Dear Mr & Mrs. Welch,

Please excuse my not answering your letter until now, but as you might well expect I've been otherwise occupied in recent weeks. As a result I'm pretty far behind these days and must try to catch up as quickly as possible.

To begin with here, I want to thank you both for all you've done for Anna and us. And especially to you, Mrs. Welch, for being so considerate as to call my parents as you did, and then to contact me by letter. I understand very well the sadness with which you wrote at that time, since I too have been feeling my share of that along with utter helplessness. By now I trust Mr. Welch has returned safely.

The last word I had from Anna was dated Apr. 23. She was absolutely desperate and had found no way at that time to get any of them out of Saigon. Of course the red tape and bribe-taking were still in effect then, which means that in the week following anything might have happened. Time was too short for me to do anything more from this end, so whatever happened in that last week was the result of Anna's own efforts probably and perhaps being at the right place at the right time.

Personally I put more faith in prayer than luck, so still hold high hopes that somehow they did succeed in getting out.

Now that Mr. Welch is undoubtedly back home, or on the way, I'd like to ask him a few questions. Did Anna receive my letter of April 15 with copies of letters I had written to the President and to Ambassador Martin? Did you and she receive my letter of April 21? Do you know what their status was at the time you left Saigon? I know how extremely occupied you must have been during that period, but perhaps you were able to help Anna and the others in some way. I pray so.

I will always be grateful for the help and friendship you gave Anna and know you did everything possible. It will never be easy to accept what had happened in S.E. Asia and to all the worthy people there who wanted to live in freedom.

What has it all been about? I only pray Anna and the others will be heard from soon. If not, I don't know what more there is to say.

Thanks for all you did.

Sincerely,
Grant S.

FLASH-MEMOIR |
HOUSE SEVEN REUNION

Originally posted on April 4, 2017

On April 2nd, 2017, nearly 42 years after the final tragic days of the Vietnam War, I had the privilege to stand before a group of people whom my father had ushered to safety. I was introduced to the 75 attendees as the daughter of the man who had made their passage to America possible.

I was grateful for the chance to speak to them after all these years. I told them how much my father had loved Vietnam and the Vietnamese people and how impassioned he was about getting them out before the country fell.

It was my honor to be welcomed to the House Seven reunion.

"I have been taken as a real friend by so many of these people that I'm nearly overwhelmed . . . I feel a very great closeness to Vietnam and the Vietnamese people. . ." he wrote to my mother in January 1974, just a few months before we, his entire family, joined him there.

I told the gathering that I wanted to use this story of my father's dedication and their escape to teach a new generation about the Vietnam Era and the importance of remembering it.

I was presented with flowers and given an energetic round of applause, and afterwards there were handshakes and hugs and photographs. Indeed, I believe I felt in that moment, as my father had, "taken as a real friend by so many of these people that I was nearly overwhelmed."

FLASH-MEMOIR |
UNEXPECTED CONNECTIONS

Originally posted on April 4, 2019

Coffee was out of the question; my schedule was just too harried. A small voice in me, however, had other ideas.

"Don't let this opportunity slip by," it said, "you could have things to talk about."

I made plans to visit Heather Mohr at her nonprofit farm, Keiki & Plow, to share ideas for building on their already successful endeavors. We stood on the startlingly steep slopes of O'ahu's Koko Crater, enjoying the broad view, the sun gentle and warm, and our talk turned to my writing projects, to Vietnam.

"My grandfather died there," she said. "In the Operation Babylift crash."

Heather Mohr's paternal grandfather, Air Force Master Sergeant Wendle Lee Payne, died on the Operation Babylift flight on April 4, 1975.

I was stunned. "I was supposed to be on that plane but my mom changed our plans at the last minute to make more room for the orphans."

Heather's paternal grandfather, Master Sergeant Wendle Lee Payne, age 46, died attempting to evacuate war orphans out of Vietnam to America.

Technically, the war had been over since '73, but the impending invasion by the North Vietnamese belied that notion. Payne was one of the few servicemen who remained in South Vietnam to facilitate the "peace" and he was an Air Force Loadmaster Technician on the C-5A aircraft designated for the initial Babylift flight.

Shortly after take-off, a mechanical malfunction caused the plane to crash, killing about half of those on board. It's difficult to find consistent casualty and survivor counts, probably because of the overriding chaos in Saigon at the time, however, what is sure is that the 17-year-old young man who would become Heather's father, lost his father that very day.

It was a miracle that my family was not on that flight as originally planned, but it would be well into adulthood until I would finally realize that I had long carried a heavy burden

Heather Mohr and I met to talk about other thing on a warm day in 2019 . . . and found we were connected by the invisible threads of history

of survivor's guilt: I grew up quietly believing that I had lived because so many of those Babylift orphans had died in my place.

As Heather and I stood there in all that beauty, the fact of the crash seemed surreal—my family's near-miss and her family's loss—and yet our conversation brought it close.

Is there any remedy for tragedy? If there is, it is in the sharing.

I resist pat answers—such as "that one coincidence put all of your far-reaching questions and qualms to rest"—but I can say that it did move something in me, gave me a deeper reason to keep exploring this American question of Vietnam, and what it means to all of us.

MY VIETNAM JOURNEY

I've been to Vietnam twice. The first time I was taken there just before I turned eight. The second time, I took myself there as a celebration on the 40th anniversary of my father's escape from his most feared enemy, the communists. I traveled with my daughter to Saigon and Phu Quoc to retrace his footsteps.

Between those times, 1975 and 2015, Vietnam haunted me. Not in-your-face horror-movie haunting, but behind-the-scenes-always-brewing haunting. The fact that I'd been one of the few American children there in those fateful months before the end of that fumbled war was never farther away than a casual conversation about where I'd grown up. Once I earned my bachelor's degree in journalism, people invariably said, "You should write about *that*."

In 2012, I was taking a casual walk through Washington Park in Albany, New York and talking on the phone with an old friend who knew my entire life story. When I mentioned my tenuous circumstances and that I was thinking of going back to writing again—but wasn't sure about what—she blurted out: "I think you should write about Vietnam."

What happened next is a little hard to explain. The air went out of me to the point where I felt as if I'd been struck by a physical wave and it took several moments before I could assure her that the choking sound coming over the phone did not mean I was in any immediate physical danger. Later, she told me that, in some strange, inexplicable coincidence, she had been looking at a stack of my father's books that I'd gifted her some time before, I was completely sold. The confluence of these circumstances

The author on Vung Tau Beach, 1974, about the time that the North Vietnamese Army was gearing up to take the South.

The author on Khem Beach, Phu Quoc Island, 2015, the day before the 40th Anniversary of her father's evacuation and The Socialist Republic of Vietnam's 40th Independence Day Celebration.

were overwhelming in my vulnerable state and it was quite clear that *not* writing about Vietnam was no longer an option.

So over the past decade, I have worked on this project. Sometimes with all the hours in my days, sometimes only in the back of my mind as jobs and other obligations were more pressing. Despite the length of time that I've been wrangling with the material, I am always surprised at how fresh and alive it all feels. I've reread my mother's and father's letters numerous times, looked over the scattered bits of paperwork and images, had numerous conversations and, nearly always, I am enveloped with a sense of wonder and awe.

The Vietnam War Era is a huge subject and I sometimes still struggle with not feeling adequate to the momentousness of it. As I wrote in my 2015 chapbook, *The Fight to Write, What the Vietnam War Taught Me About Truth and Writing*:

> Millions of words have been written about the Vietnam War. I was scared to write my stories because they are such a small piece of something so big.
>
> In the film documentary, *The Vietnam War—an Intimate History*, Ken Burns describes the it as "a tragedy of epic proportions that took the lives of 58,000 Americans, as many as three million Vietnamese, polarized American society as nothing has since the Civil War, fundamentally challenged Americans' faith in our leaders, our government,

and many of our most respected institutions, and called into question the belief in our own exceptionalism."

But as I keep writing, I am finding that my stories are meaningful and they do add to the conversation.

I am finding that my fears are real but that they are worth overcoming.

I am finding that I am glad I keep fighting to write.

Vietnam is a wound that is still bleeding. Our country, our world is bleeding, as it has throughout history. Is it your fault? No. Is it your responsibility to fix these things? I don't believe so.

Is it your responsibility to find out what all this means to you?

I believe it is.

My chapbook *The Fight to Write* explores the power of writing.

NOTES

Great effort has been made to trace and acknowledge owners of copyrighted materials; however, the author would be pleased to add, correct, or revise any such acknowledgements in future printings.

Prologue

Charles Eugene Taber. 2003. *Get out Any Way You Can.* Infinity Publishing. In addition to Taber's account, I used the notes and letters my father wrote on Phu Quoc Island and aboard *The American Challenger*; an official account submitted to the bureau by the radio technician Don Gass; and interviews with select Vietnamese staff.

My Father's Plaque

"VietnamOnline.com - Vietnam Travel & Living Guide." n.d. www. vietnamonline.com. https://www.vietnamonline.com.

Epigraph

Drury, Bob, and Tom Clavin. 2012. *Last Men Out.* Simon and Schuster.

Photo: Saigon 1960s Street Scene

manhhai. 2023. "01. KỶ NIỆM 160 NĂM Ngày Sứ Đoàn Phan Thanh Giản Lên Đường Sang Pháp và Tây Ban Nha (21-6-1863 - 21-6-2023)." Flickr. June 20, 2023. https://www.flickr.com/photos/13476480@N07/.

Photo: Aerial shot of 7 Hong Thap Tu Street

manhhai. 2017. "Nhà Số 7 Hồng Thập Tự - Đài Phát Thanh Tâm Lý Chiến 'Mẹ Việt Nam' Của CIA." Flickr. April 1, 2017. https://www.flickr.com/photos/13476480@N07/32928480734.

Photo: Nixon in China

Byron E. Schumaker, ca. 1935-, Photographer (NARA record: 8451340), Public domain, via Wikimedia Commons

2023. Wikimedia.org. 2023. https://upload.wikimedia.org/wikipedia/commons/3/32/President_and_Mrs._Nixon_visit_the_Great_Wall_of_China.jpg.

Photo: Kissinger close-up

pingnews.com. 2006. "Public Domain: Henry Kissinger on the Phone to Brent Scowcroft, April 29, 1975 by David Hume Kennerly (NARA)." Flickr. October 20, 2006. https://www.flickr.com/photos/pingnews/274991009.

Photo: JFK Picture

2014. Wikimedia.org. 2014. https://upload.wikimedia.org/wikipedia/commons/3/3a/JFKBerlinSpeech.jpg.

Photo: Pan Am Plane

Aero Icarus. 1989. "Pan Am Boeing 747-100; N748PA@ZRH, June 1989/ACI." Flickr. June 1, 1989. https://www.flickr.com/photos/aero_icarus/8169130981.

Photo: Oval Office Meeting

Photograph of President Ford Meeting with Secretary of State Henry Kissinger, Army Chief of Staff General Frederick Weyand, and Graham Martin, Ambassador to Vietnam, in the Oval Office.

David Hume Kennerly, Public domain, via Wikimedia Commons

2023. Wikimedia.org. 2023. https://upload.wikimedia.org/wikipedia/commons/3/38/President_Ford_meets_with_Kissinger%2C_Weyand%2C_and_Martin_-_NARA_-_186794.jpg.

Photo: Paris Peace Agreement

Picture of the "Agreement" copy on ending war and restoring peace in Vietnam. Picture taken at the National Air and Space Museum's Steven F. Udvar-Hazy Center in Chantilly, Virginia, USA.

Acharya, Sanjay. 2017. "English: Picture of the 'Agreement' Copy on Ending War and Restoring Peace in Vietnam. Picture Taken at the National Air and Space Museum's Steven F. Udvar-Hazy Center in Chantilly, Virginia, USA." Wikimedia Commons. December 28, 2017. https://commons.wikimedia.org/w/index.php?curid=74798041.

Photo: Duc Hotel

"LÊ QUÝ ĐÔN KHUNG TRỜI KỶ NIỆM." n.d. Accessed June 20, 2023. http://thaolqd.blogspot.com/2013/03/vunglan-can-truong-tiep-theo-bay-gio-ta.html.

My Vietnam Journey

"The Vietnam War." n.d. Ken Burns. Accessed June 19, 2023. https://www.kenburns.com/films/vietnam/.

"Watch the Vietnam War | a Film by Ken Burns & Lynn Novick | PBS | Ken Burns." n.d. The Vietnam War: A Film by Ken Burns & Lynn Novick | PBS. https://www.pbs.org/kenburns/the-vietnam-war/.

End of a Nation

Glenn, Tom. 2015. Review of *Bitter Memories: The Fall of Saigon, April 1975. Studies in Intelligence*, Vol. 59, No. 4, December 2015.

Photo: Landing Craft Units

U.S. Navy photo by Photographer's Mate 3rd Class Jeremy L. Grisham, Public domain, via Wikimedia Commons

2023. Wikimedia.org. 2023. https://upload.wikimedia.org/wikipedia/commons/7/7b/US_Navy_060606-N-8154G-115_Two_Landing_Craft_Utilities_%28LCU%29_assigned_to_Amphibious_Craft_Unit_Two_%28ACU-2%29%2C_rehearse_storming_the_beach_in_Curacao%2C_Netherlands_Antilles.jpg.

Photo: South Vietnamese Soldiers

> US military personnel, Public domain, via Wikimedia Commons
> 2023. Wikimedia.org. 2023. https://upload.wikimedia.org/wikipedia/commons/4/40/ARVN_Rangers_defend_Saigon%2C_Tet_Offensive.jpg.

House Seven Operations

> Review of *Vietnam Order of Battle*. n.d. https://www.pyswarrior.com/VietnamOBPSYOP.html.

The CIA

> "Welcome to the CIA Web Site — Central Intelligence Agency." 2018. Cia.gov. 2018. https://www.cia.gov.

Trained for Psychological Warfare

> Pruitt, Sarah. 2016. "OSS: The Predecessor of the CIA." HISTORY. October 28, 2016. https://www.history.com/news/oss-the-predecessor-of-the-cia.
> "China and the USA." 2019. Johndclare.net. 2019. https://www.johndclare.net/China12.htm.

The V-12 program

> "The V-12 Officer Training Program." n.d. Public2.Nhhcaws.local. https://www.history.navy.mil/browse-by-topic/wars-conflicts-and-operations/world-war-ii/1942/manning-the-us-navy/v-12-program.html.

Henry Kissinger

> History.com Editors. 2018. "Henry A. Kissinger." HISTORY. August 21, 2018. https://www.history.com/topics/cold-war/henry-kissinger.
> Wikipedia Contributors. 2019. "Henry Kissinger." Wikipedia. Wikimedia Foundation. July 26, 2019. https://en.wikipedia.org/wiki/Henry_Kissinger.
> "The Vietnam War in Forty Quotes." n.d. Council on Foreign Relations. Accessed June 19, 2023. http://www.cfr.org/blog/vietnam-war-forty-quotes.

The Domino Theory

> "The New Frontier, Great Society, and Vietnam War - Ppt Download." n.d. Slideplayer.com. Accessed June 19, 2023. https://slideplayer.com/slide/4251162/.

JFK's Famous Berlin Speech

> "Kennedy Delivering His 'Ich Bin Ein Berliner' Speech, 1963 - Rare Historical Photos." 2016. Https://Rarehistoricalphotos.com/. October 29, 2016. https://www.rarehistoricalphotos.com/kennedy-ich-bin-ein-berliner-1963/.

Why Were Families in a Warzone?

> Charles Eugene Taber. 2003. *Get out Any Way You Can*. Infinity Publishing.
> Review of Vietnam: *A Television History*. 1997. *WGBH Educational Foundation*.

President Nixon's speech

"January 23, 1973: Address to the Nation Announcing an Agreement on Ending the War in Vietnam | Miller Center." 2016. Millercenter.org. October 20, 2016. https://www.millercenter.org/the-presidency/presidential-speeches/january-23-1973-address-nation-announcing-agreement-ending-war

Kissinger quote re June 1973

Channel, History. 2017. "Vietnam: A Television History (Ep-12) the End of the Tunnel." *YouTube*. https://www.youtube.com/watch?v=dSPdd4rMwMU.

Kat Fitzpatrick at House Seven Reunion

Photo courtesy of John Phan

Kat Fitzpatrick on Khem Beach

Photo by Chelsea Gandy

The Nung Guards

Onion, Rebecca. 2013. "A Forgotten Chapter of Vietnam: How an Indigenous Tribe Won the Admiration of the Green Berets—and Lost Everything Else." Slate Magazine. November 27, 2013. https://slate.com/news-and-politics/2013/11/the-green-berets-and-the-montagnards-how-an-indigenous-tribe-won-the-admiration-of-green-berets-and-lost-everything.html.

Staff. n.d. "The Chinese Nungs." Special Forces Chapter 78. Accessed June 21, 2023. https://www.specialforces78.com/the-chinese-nungs/.

> **Photo:** "Talking with a Nung Sentry (Nung Mercenaries Were Used as Guards at Many Special Forces Camps) At ..." n.d. Www.awm.gov.au. Accessed June 21, 2023. https://www.awm.gov.au/collection/C309064.

Graham Greene

timdolinghcmc@gmail.com. 2014. "Graham Greene's Saigon." HISTORIC VIETNAM. January 15, 2014. https://www.historicvietnam.com/graham-greenes-saigon-revisited/.

Paris Peace Accords

Snepp, Frank. 1977. *Decent Interval*. Random House (NY).

Viet Cong Name Origin

History.com Editors. 2019. "National Liberation Front Formed." HISTORY. June 7, 2019. https://www.history.com/this-day-in-history/national-liberation-front-formed.

Battle of Ban Me Thuot

Veith, George J. 2013. *Black April: The Fall of South Vietnam, 1973-1975*. New York: Encounter Books.

Snepp, Frank. 1977. *Decent Interval*. Random House (NY).

Photo: Phoenix Study Group "Campus"

https://www.facebook.com/photo/?fbid=5298892043500619&set=gm.10160795220139113&idorvanity=104774824112

Photo: Nixon Photo (Flashing the Vs)

Ollie Atkins, White House photographer, Public domain, via Wikimedia Commons, 2023. Wikimedia.org. 2023. https://upload.wikimedia.org/wikipedia/commons/2/21/NIXONcampaigns.jpg.

Nixon Resignation Letter

Richard M. Nixon Resignation Letter, 08/09/1974, Record Group 59: General Records of the Department of State, 1756 | 1979, NARA, College Park, MD. (ARC #302035)

A Clarifying Note

O'Brien, Tim. 1998. *The Things They Carried*. Demco Media.

Photo: Black cloud over Saigon during 1968 Tet Offensive

Review of *Black Smoke Covers Areas of the Capital City and Fire Trucks Rush to the Scenes of Fires Set during Attacks by the Viet Cong during the Festive Tet Holiday Period. Saigon, 1968*. n.d. Series: Miscellaneous Vietnam Photographs. National Archives. Accessed July 20, 2023. https://catalog.archives.gov/id/541874?objectPage=3.

Photo: October Demonstrations

Ut, Nick. 1974. *As Smoke Billows from a Burning Motorcycle, South Vietnamese Riot Police Face Several Thousand Angry Protesters Who Were Trying to Move Their Anti-Corruption Demonstration from Suburban Saigon to the Center of the City on Oct. 31, 1974*. AP.

ACKNOWLEDGEMENTS

The work on this project has spanned over a decade, so I was initially daunted at the prospect of putting my many thanks in order. However, once I remembered that the best place to start is always at home, the words just flowed.

I can't but help thanking my dad for being who he was, for writing me letters when I was but a wee lass, for bestowing a special nickname upon me (to be revealed in a more intimate memoir someday), for nurturing the connection between us, and of course for having the temperament and courage to be the kind of man who would "stick with his collaborators" and see them to safety.

Then there's my mom, who as one of my MFA mentors, said, "turned out to be a real hero in this story, too." Her letters provide not only context to our 10 months in Saigon but also humor, perspective, and quite simply, love. How she kept up with seven kids plus writing regular letters etc, etc, I'll never know. She was my cheerleader and my inspiration, and I'll always be sorry that I did not get to spend more time with her than I did.

Many thanks to all my siblings, especially to Marina and Chris, for the countless conversations trying to make sense of our disparate and spotty memories. And to Mikey for digitizing all of my parents' ephemera, thus keeping the information safe and making it accessible. Thanks also to Jimmy for reading some of my drafts early on and sending me encouraging comments.

The preservation of this story and these memories, I often feel, will be of most benefit to the coming generations. I'm so grateful to my daughter, Chelsea, for jumping in to accompany me to Vietnam in 2015, turning what felt like a potentially emotionally arduous trip into a warm and much more humorous journey. Thank you to my son Dylan for spending many happy hours discussing writing and plot and story with me and helping me bring much of the Phu Quoc evacuation scene into clear focus.

My cousin Laurel Williams has held the torch for this project for so long that I cannot recall our first conversation about it. Many thanks to her for always being there to cheer me on and offer insights and feedback. Her support has been invaluable.

Thanks also to her mom, my dad's sister, for the many hours she spent with me sharing stories of my father's childhood and the correspondence he sent to her over the years.

Without my dear friend Maggie McLaughlin, I may never have gotten the message that I really had to take up my pen and do this project. It was she, in 2012, who uttered the words "I think you should write about Vietnam," at just the right time for them to wash over me like an outside set. Thank you, Maggie, for playing that key role. And of course for knocking it out of the park with the design of this edition. It's fun to be in the same lineup again after all these years.

A special thank you to Marine Corps veteran Jim Brown for the many, many deep and also delightful conversations that gave me a soldier's insight into the war.

I would also like to thank the staff, faculty, and students of the Solstice MFA Creative Writing Program for all the inspiration, support, guidance, and companionship, especially David Yoo, who nimbly served as my intrepid Sancho Panza.

Additionally, I'm grateful to Crandall Public Library in Glens Falls, N.Y., where I spent many hours while working on my master's thesis. A special shout-out to the Memory Sharing Group, to the storytelling class at the Folklife Center, and to those who attended my writing classes.

Cảm ơn to the House Seven Vietnamese community, many of whom embraced me like a family member.

Michael Erickson was a font of Phoenix Study Group information. His initial email efforts led to Kim Westlake-Life's formation of the Facebook Group, allowing us "alum" to keep in touch and exchange valuable information and memories. This led to my re-acquaintance with the PSG librarian Karen Griffith Kaiser which has proven to be a most inspiring connection.

Thanks to good friend and writer Paul Block for reviewing the manuscript and inspiring me with confidence.

A big hug to "my other favorite son" Roberto Belanger for using his eagle eye on the final proof.

A *"danke"* is deserved by Anne-Marie Baker for benevolently schooling me on German spelling and grammar. And to Elyn Zimmerman, Jana Vandelaar JP, and Nanson Serriane—your long-standing belief in me and this project heartened me over the years.

A shout out also to Don Ritner whose invitation to be a featured speaker at his 2022 YES Salon in Troy, N.Y. helped reinvigorate my dedication to this project.

Last but not least, a heartfelt hug to my wide, loose circle of friends and family the world over. (Loose modifying circle, not friends.) Thank you for understanding when I said, "No, I can't come out to play, my writing desk is calling," for your long-enduring encouragement, and for the serendipitous support at the moments I needed it the most.

ABOUT THE AUTHOR

 KAT FITZPATRICK was one of the few American dependents living in Saigon at the end of the Vietnam War, the daughter of a CIA operative who worked in ultra-secret propaganda. Her first experience with writing came when she took a page from her mother's book and corresponded regularly with her father while he was away on assignment. The spell of the writing life never released her and she earned two degrees—a Journalism B.A. and a Creative Writing M.F.A—in allegiance to the call. She balances the emotionally challenging work of writing about the Vietnam Era with a not-quite-murder mystery series featuring the accidental-gumshoe Kat Mandu. She lives in Upstate N.Y. where she escapes from her desk on a semi-regular basis by running, hiking, and kayaking. Visit her online at Kat-Fitzpatrick.com.